To Peter

A Minority of One

with love
Lesley.

Lesley Brain's
story of her time in the Big Brother house

Grosvenor House
Publishing Limited

This book is published by
Grosvenor House Publishing Ltd
28-30 High Street, Guildford, Surrey, GU1 3HY.
www.grosvenorhousepublishing.co.uk

A CIP record for this book
is available from the British Library

ISBN 978-1-906210-61-8

Printed in Great Britain by Biddles Ltd, King's Lynn, Norfolk

George Orwell states in his book 'Nineteen Eighty-Four' that being in a minority, even a minority of one, does not necessarily mean that you are mad.

On May 30th, 2007 twelve women entered the Big Brother house in the eighth series of the British version of what is a worldwide annual phenomenon.

I was one of those women. Since coming home I have been asked why I did it and what it was like. This is my account of those nine days, eleven hours and forty-one minutes, and of the months leading up to them.

It has taken 18 days to write and was completed before the programme finished. Having no record of the series I have had to rely solely on my memory of events and conversations. I have tried, too, to recall precisely my thoughts during those times. Though I am sure it is largely accurate I apologise if anything I attribute to anyone else is not also precisely what was said. This is the original copy with one exception. Because I used quotations from Orwell's 'Nineteen Eighty Four', threading them through the text to show the remarkable similarities and connections between book and show, I approached the agent who handles his 'permissions'. Initially this was granted, only to be followed later by the statement that permissions are not granted that are in any way connected to the Big Brother television programme. All extracts have been removed.

Big Brother comes in many guises.

There have been many people who have supported me in my mad venture to whom I should like to say thank you. They include my family and friends, of course, and the people of Tetbury and Gloucestershire. I am grateful, too, for the kindness of strangers.

This book is for David.

'They are lovely people and they are infuriating people.'

Lesley Brain

CHAPTER ONE

I blame it all on Andrew Marr. I want to meet him and it's proving impossible. I could never understand why the late Princess Diana wasn't happy and claimed to be bored alone in Kensington Palace. All she had to do was to lift the telephone and invite anyone, anyone at all, for lunch and no one, no politician, popstar, prince, would decline. I would invite Andrew Marr, but not being a world famous princess and icon I am struggling to engineer a meeting. Perhaps if I were an unlikely 'celebrity', albeit a modern, five-minute version, he would want to interview me. It's worth a chance. So, celebrity it is then.

We have just returned from six years living in Portugal and are basking, not in the sun as this is January, but in the relief of being Home. Not that we were ever the sort of ex-pats who having chosen to live abroad spend each day in a drunken state of sentimental reminiscences about what they have left behind. It has always baffled me how the Scottish in particular speak so highly of their homeland but rarely choose to live there. But it was never our intention to stay in that inoffensive country for so long or to suffer the company of the British who live there; these people are proof that travel does not necessarily broaden the mind. We are still at the stage of skipping with delight around the aisles at Tescos and Waitrose, marvelling at the ease of everyday conversations, and glorying in the lushness of the Gloucestershire countryside. So green. A colour hard even for the dictionary to define. 'Somewhere between yellow and blue.' A colour that absurdly brings to mind the word 'god'.

Despite our view that everyone should be sent abroad for six years the better to appreciate England, we are revelling in the comfort of our new home. However, David and I are strangers to the concept of contentment. No sooner has Pickfords, or whoever, disgorged our belongings into a little piece of paradise in Tetbury than we are looking around for our next adventure. Despite or because of the marching of time we cannot afford to stand still. There is also a lot of catching up to be done.

The cultural desert from which we have newly returned has made us thirsty and if we have one certain enemy in our battle to experience variety it is time, which slips away at an alarming rate. In reading magazines and newspapers to find out 'what's on' I am struck by this new phenomenon of celebrity that has swept the country in our absence. Not the celebrity that goes with talent whether it be the kicking of a football, the perform-ance of a pop song or the absurdity of a walk down a catwalk, but the whatever does or did she do, the sort of celebrity where the origins of the seed of fame are lost forever in the branches and tentacles of modern media, in the bibles of Hello and Heat and all their myriad chums. Then each year there is that Mecca of wannabees, that three month long jamboree of instant fame: the television programme, Big Brother.

We go to live in Portugal and, spookily, simultaneously Big Brother is launched in Britain, and throughout the world it seems, and every day for three months each year some four million plus people view the show each day and follow its every nuance compulsively. And celebrities are born or created. Apparently. I have never seen the programme myself but feel that I have. Despite the viewing figures, this is a furtive activity. Everyone knows about it but no one has ever seen it. A bit like God and the wind, or Cliff Richard. Love it, or hate it, it is HUGE. It cannot be ignored. Or at least that is what I decide.

The programme, it seems, is a voyeurism fest where 12 or so 'housemates' with nothing discernable in common and nothing better to do are locked in a specially constructed 'house' and filmed 24 hours a day. Over a period of 13 weeks viewers vote on who should be evicted and who should stay to win a one hundred thousand pounds cash prize.

I know nothing more about the form of the television show but feel myself to be fully qualified for untalented celebrity being a person who is omni-incompetent. So it is with complete confidence I join the very long line of hopefuls at the Cardiff Big Brother auditions in January 2007. I am not a stranger to Cardiff. During our time in Bath David and I were drawn to the idea of playing bingo. The appeal lay in the potential huge winnings and the way the game was being newly glamorised. This was before Sharon Osborne took over this, and the rest of the media universe, but David and I are often ahead of our time. We approached our new career of bingoists with our usual thoroughness. We went to Weston Super Mare to practice before releasing ourselves on the bigger fish of Cardiff. Suffice it to say that I found the game harder than I had expected and I would not have been able to play at all had it not been for the string-vested dustbin man sitting next to me who gallantly, and literally, held my hand and taught me the rules. As it was, my confusion and questions led to the 'caller' falling about in hysterical laughter and having to be replaced by a sterner reserve, and I was given a huge bar of chocolate and asked to leave. Undeterred by this unpromising debut David and I presented ourselves at the glossy new building in Cardiff for a more glamorous and hopefully more rewarding game. To our chagrin we were asked if we were members and refused entry. We are unused to this and so the manager was called. He explained that references would be required. I asked what nature of referee and since we did not know anyone who was already a member he accepted that a bank would be appropriate. I gave him our Coutts private banker as contact. At this the manager looked very doubtful asking if it were a building society but two weeks later our membership card duly arrived and, bingo, we were off. What Coutts must have thought I don't know but if they, or we, had hoped it would make our fortune we would all have been most disappointed. I never really got the hang of it and to this day still hold the record for the most False Calls in a bingo hall.

Despite this I am confident in my application for the Big Brother game. This confidence is based on my knowledge of the book from which the show's concept originates. I feel, too, a certain affinity with its' author on the tenuous basis that as I was being born in the coldest February of all time in 1947 George Orwell sat down to start writing 'Nineteen Eighty Four'. Records do not show if the two events were linked in some way but sixty years later they are to merge in one neat, satisfying circle.

'Nineteen Eighty Four' is simple story told in a spare, elegant style – a story of loneliness, defiance, forbidden and furtive sex and of deadly terror. I am five hours queuing in the bitter January cold outside Cardiff's impressive if Stalinist town hall. I have ample time to remind myself of the book. In my naivety I am certain that the subsequent interview will require an in-depth knowledge of the inspiration for the programme and I need to be intellectually alert in order to compete. Perhaps I am confusing this with Mastermind. Looking around I have reason to doubt that we are all equally prepared or have the same expectations. One girl is particularly prominent in that, despite the near freezing conditions, she has been decisive in what she has chosen to wear, unlike the others who look like they have just donned what came to hand by their bedsides that morning. I, after a lot of thought, have opted for a cashmere roll neck sweater, straight woollen trousers, an Armani jacket and a long Max Mara coat with leather trim – all in black but enlivened by an orange crushed velvet scarf. This is a bold gesture, the orange, as I have recently had a girlie day with a friend that included colour counselling and was told by a hatchet faced woman wearing beige that I must never wear orange. She said it fiercely, darkly, with her breath so close to my face that I am tempted to return the compliment and recommend mouthwash. But I am a rebel and, never having worn orange before, I am now obliged to seek it out whenever possible. Anyway the effect is practical, elegant and warm with, I hope, a touch of class.

By contrast the decisive girl has opted for nothing. She is completely naked. Not unreasonably in the light of the cold she has taken to running and jumping and generally showing herself off to the assembled and, it seemed to me, indifferent crowd. I guess there are a thousand people queuing. None is as brave or as blue.

The people around me are hardened and experienced auditionees. I am the only wannabee virgin. They want to chat so I conclude that they and the nude girl – apparently there are always naked girls at auditions and they are never 'chosen', an insight I offer for any others who might see this as a route to success – are totally confident in their literary knowledge. We get talking. I meet transvestites, transsexuals, homosexuals, the obese, a girl with razor cuts up her arm, teenagers with babies. I am surprised by how readily and openly they label themselves. It's not something I am comfortable with – this narrow tabloid description of oneself. I rather hope that I am too complex a person to be so easily pigeonholed. Everyone is friendly and they openly conclude that I am a loving and supportive parent holding a place for some absent young relative. As we talk there is support for the novel idea that I should audition in my own right. I do not disabuse them. I am a Johnny-come-lately. Some are on their seventh year of auditioning for this show – and any other talent shows that come to Cardiff – and as seasoned auditionees do not see the correlation being their recidivist behaviour and its attendant failure. Some talk confidently and knowledgeably albeit in hushed whispers about the audition process. One girl – bi-sexual, she tells me – got as far as London and 'then never heard again'. We are in awe of her achievement.

Perhaps she didn't know the book well enough. To avoid this I run over the plot in my mind.

It is 1984 – remember Orwell is writing sixty years ago and this is science fiction -and in London which is called Airstrip One in the state of Oceania. This is a superpower controlled by the restrictive 'Party' which is led by its symbolic head, Big Brother. There is no law and only one rule – absolute obedience in act and thought. I look around at my fellow auditionees and think this might suit them very well as, with the exception of the naked girl, they seem pretty short of both deed and thought and, in truth, despite her running and jumping I can't really imagine that she is doing much thinking.

Oceanian society is divided hierarchically into three groups: a privileged Inner Party, a subservient Outer Party and a sunken mass of 'proles'. I feel myself most drawn by nature to the Inner Party but acknowledge that my standing here in the bitter cold for five hours might neatly have established me as a 'prole'.

The hero of the book is Winston Smith. He is a member of the Outer Party and is employed at the Ministry of Truth as a falsifier of records. I am not drawn to Winston finding him too wet for my liking and my natural snobbishness inclines me towards the Inner Party who I suspect lead a life more akin to my own, but I am already inclined to think that my own finely honed skill as a 'falsifier of records' may stand me in good stead in this 'celebrity' business. Despite my poor opinion of him Winston resists all pressure to conform and secretly reacts against it. He meets Julia, a non-intellectual, who conveniently for Winston believes in sex and they engage in an illicit affair. Emboldened by this, Winston approaches a high ranking Inner Party official, O'Brien, and who, foolishly in my opinion as you should never entirely trust anyone from a different class from oneself, asks him to put them in touch with Big Brother's arch enemy. The encouragement they receive from O'Brien turns out to be a transparent ploy. (I like O'Brien but then I am drawn to life's winners). I am unsurprised by this but it wouldn't be much of a story otherwise so I'm with Orwell on this. Anyway Winston is one of life's losers so it's all in character. The two lovers are arrested, separated, interrogated and tortured. They betray each other and are finally liquidated.

Not for the first time I wonder why I am here.

What will be intriguing is how closely <u>this</u> Big Brother follows the principles and execution of the first.

The queue moves and at last I am inside the building. The hundreds and hundreds of waiting contestants are orderly and largely silent which makes me wonder about the security guards who patrol our compliant lines. I ask the others, the more Knowing Ones, what they, the guards, expect to happen and am told, darkly, that in previous years 'there has been trouble'. Trouble. Bored, I am hopeful.

Suddenly it's all happening. As the queue progresses we are divided into groups of eight and given simple children's games to play. I am deemed successful at passing a ball down a line of people and pass on to a group where each of must name an item we would put into Room 101. Cunningly I combine two items by naming the colour orange and Easyjet and I suggest that environmental damage would be limited if both were banned.

I am aware by now that I am one of the more extraordinary contestants by virtue of age – it is rare to see anyone over 25 – and verbal skills. When asked to say a few things about herself one young hopeful confines herself to saying she has 'three kids'. Not, I would have thought, the perfect recommendation for a venture that would mean being away from home for three months. The 8 members of my group, with whom I have now bonded, are asked to extend their hands and those deemed suitable to stay have their hands stamped with an inky eye. The Big Brother Eye. So Big Brother's eye is not on a screen on every wall but on the back of our hands.

This reminds me of my school days and that terrible business of choosing or being chosen. That time when we all stood in line and the teacher or more superior pupil picked people for the school play or sports team. We stood rigid with apprehension. There were those who feared being chosen and those who were terrified of not being chosen. I assume that like so many of my life's early lessons the procedure has now been banned on the grounds of competitiveness and therefore cruelty. Well, even then in the far off days of childhood I wanted to be chosen. Pick me. Pick me. Better still I aspired then, as now, to do the choosing.

My reaction to the smudgy black eye on the back of MY hand amazed me then and now. I jump up and down and wave my arms and shriek and whoop. I am thrilled. And more than that. In that moment I know for certain that I will be chosen. I look into the blurred eye looking back at me from my hand and know that whatever is ahead I, like Winston before his final liquidation, will learn to love Big Brother.

I am given a number to wear. 101. I am number 101. The number of the dreaded 'Nineteen Eighty Four' room that holds all we most fear and hate. It cannot be a coincidence.

I had expected the atmosphere at auditions to be frivolous, fun, even electric. Apart from Nude Girl, with whom I am now feeling some curious bond, the overwhelming feeling in the room is of tension and anxiety. This is a game show, I want to cry out. Where is the carnival atmosphere? All around me I see gritted teeth and a steely resolve as though we search for the Holy Grail. Instead of the expected attention-grabbing exhibitionists the faces around me are listless, apathetic, conforming...nothing is explained to us; we are herded by young Big Brother organisers who are so alike they might as well be wearing masks and uniforms; we are already part of the sausage-making, bureaucratic, humour-free machine that is Oceania. Still I look down at my eye-stamped hand and feel enormous pride. Not yet time to step off the machine.

I am sitting on a bar stool in a small black cardboard booth. Strong lights are shining on me but I can just make out two girls seated in the dark with clipboards. I am being filmed. The questions are dull and random. Except I already know that nothing here, least of all myself, is spontaneous. I want to say 'You know you want me. Why don't we just agree that I shall turn up at the studio in Elstree in the summer and that way we save ourselves a lot of bother?' I don't know why they didn't listen to me. It all might have gone so very differently if they had.

I am seated in a room with perhaps thirty other people. Is this all that is left of us? Have the others been liquidated? In front of me is a questionnaire.

Let me declare my hand here. I love questionnaires. I approach people with clipboards in their hands and am disappointed to be so seldom in the required demographic segment. Perhaps this stems from an early experience with my mother. It must have been the mid fifties and a timid girl, ill suited for her task, approaches my mother and asks if she will sign a petition. My mother is always generous with her opinions. 'What's it for?' 'It is pro-abortion.' My mother seizes the board from the girl who has reason to be fearful. She, my mother that is, is wearing her best astrakhan coat, always a worrying sign, and not looking the least like a pro-abortionist. She signs her name with gusto declaring, 'Abortion shouldn't just be legal, it should be compulsory.' With that she sweeps off with me flying through the air attached to her hand.

I grasp the Big Brother questionnaire and even I am daunted. 50 pages, hundreds of questions. I look at my watch. There have been hours of queuing and waiting in corridors. It's late, I'm tired and, if I'm honest, a little bored with it already but I put down my pen and take the time to think.

There is a fundamental decision to be made now. Do I tell the truth? I am after all following in the footsteps of Winston – Smith, not Churchill – who worked for the Ministry of Truth (i.e. lies) as a professional teller of lies. I, too, am qualified for this having been accused by those who don't understand me of telling lies. David, always ready to defend me behind my back, has said that I do not lie but like that other Winston, Churchill, am adept at exaggerating the truth. My overwhelming feeling is that these faceless strangers who devised, built and run this machinery of so-called entertainment and are already manipulating and controlling my day are not morally entitled to The Truth. This is not a court of law and I am answerable to no one except myself and those close to me. There's the rub. But there's no time for the moral maze. The others in the room are already hunched over their papers and since we are told nothing I do not know if this is a timed exercise. I decide to take each question on its merit.

Being 59 rather than 20, like everyone else in the room, I have more material to sift through in my head. The questions are diverse and intriguing.

I am asked to describe my mother. This <u>should</u> be easy. My sister, who has taken to the fad of life-laundry like an old washerwoman, has recently sent me a box of family letters, photographs and schoolbooks. In a school report I see that at 12 'Lesley shows off in Latin.' While this makes my sister, who is younger and more combatative, rather cross with me I am predictably pleased with myself...ego amo, or some such. I have very little memory of schooldays except of tedium and total incomprehension. The whole sorry business of my schooldays could have been conducted in Swedish for all I ever understood of it. I went to the same school as others who have written of it – Sheila Hancock, Diana Quick – and from their glowing descriptions I can't recognise the unimaginative, narrow-minded, bullied and bullying experience that is my secondary education. In the box my sister has sent, however, there is not a trace of my mother. This should not surprise me. She was completely non-materialistic in herself, though not for others, and apart from her lack of religious belief and dislike of women, per-fectly suited to the life of a nun in an enclosed order. In any case, preferring to present herself as an enigma, whatever she might have possessed she will have destroyed. So I look to my most recent experience of my mother for clues as to how to describe her.

David had lived and worked for many years in Bath before we met there. We decided when he 'retired', which like Frank Sinatra he does on a regular basis before the lure of the draw-ing board, Siren-like, calls to him, we should perhaps move away to pastures new and we began house-hunting. We were open-minded. Always a mistake. We looked at a fisherman's cottage in Southwold, a loft apartment in Soho, a country estate in Scotland even. Then we had a trip to Cornwall. We viewed a wonderful house almost at the edge of my known world, another mile and we would have been in America. A Japanese house, all wood and space and light.

Returning from the viewing we crossed the Fal on the King Harry ferry which we had never done before. 'We shall stop for coffee. There is a restaurant just round the corner.' Instinct, not knowledge, but I'm good at this. A boyfriend once said that if he were lost in the Sahara he would want to be lost with me as I would be the one person who would find a Michelin-starred restaurant round the corner. 'Take the sharp turning to the left and down the lane. We shall park there and walk down.' Authority unhampered by knowledge – my best skill. As we stepped from the car it was then my mother chose to make an appearance and I remarked to David, 'Be careful what you say. My Mother is with us.' We commented later how natural this seemed to both of us. Surprising but natural, given that she had died five years earlier. She looked as she always looked, a blue chiffon scarf round her neck floating out in the breeze. We walked down to the restaurant, a thatched building by the river, with a collection of wartime memorabilia in the garden. It was from that spot that Americans had set off for the French coast towards the end of the war. Inside a girl was laying up a delicious looking buffet lunch. I asked if we were too late for coffee. There was much activity in the kitchen but we were the only customers. She smiled at us. A pretty girl, probably a student making money in the holiday season. It would be no trouble and we should take a seat. We sat in a corner, quietly talking about our future. (David, like me, lives in the future and the past, in spite of having so much of it, doesn't engage too much of his thoughts.)

Soon the girl came back carrying a tray with a cafatiere and three cups and saucers. Placing it on the rustic table she asked, 'Where is the other lady?' I told her there was no other lady, just the two of us. She was quite insistent. No, there was another lady. An older lady. A lady with a blue scarf. She began to be agitated. She suspected something amiss. She went off in the direction of the lavatory perhaps to check for herself. When she came back she was clearly in no mood to let it go. Should I have told her that what she saw was my mother who had died five years ago and for some reason of her own had decided to appear to us all on that day? We poured cold milk into our coffee and left as quickly as possible. We heard the girl telling people in the kitchen, 'I know there was another lady. An older lady. A blue scarf.'

My mother would have liked the blue scarf detail. She once said of me with a sigh, 'How much easier it would be for us all if Lesley were able to tie a scarf in a pussy cat bow!' We drove away and agreed that the most remarkable thing about the whole incident was how truly unremarkable it had seemed to us. We decide to tell no one as while we concede that we are both mad we are not mad In That Way.

For inspiration I turn back to Nineteen Eighty Four and think about my mother's Room 101. She hated –

Funerals and the hypocrisy surrounding them – she had no funeral herself and expressed the hope that she would die on a Thursday when the bins were emptied and she could go out with the rubbish.

Old people, 'People should be taken out at 60 and shot.'

The Church of England, though she had fewer objections to Quakers, Mormons and Jehovah's Witnesses believing them to be at least sincere.

Holidays. She never had one.

The colour green. She felt that God had 'overused' it in Nature.

George Formby and Hitler, in that order.

Like all the women in my family she had one weakness and that was for handsome men...fortunately my father was the best looking man she ever met and they adored each other. Struggling to condense the essence of this woman into the small box and three adjectives allocated to 'mother' I am interrupted by the girl on my right.

There has been much sighing and moaning from her which I have chosen to ignore. Since that moment, just hours ago that seems like weeks when I joined the queue outside Cardiff's town hall and gave my life to the Big Brother organisation, I have chosen to assume that I am being observed. This might be by cameras, overt or hidden, by the silent and unforthcoming stewards or by fellow potential contestants. I have decided to trust no one.

The girl next to me cries 'Can you 'elp me?' Perhaps this is part of a test to see if I am kind and helpful. Reluctantly I put down my pen and turn to her. She is beautiful. Her rough emery board voice is at odds with her achingly gorgeous face but it is her chest that most engages me. It is huge and heaving. I want to reach out a finger and test its texture and prodability. Mindful of ever-watching Big Brother I restrain myself. 'What is it?' I say in a carefully designed neutral voice. 'They're asking if I'm moggy-moose.' A tear runs down her cheek and I watch, mesmerised, as it plops onto her breast. I can see why so far she has successfully climbed the ladder of faux celebrity. 'I'm sorry?' 'They want to know if I'm moggy-moose.'

Dragging my mind away from my mother, who I suspect would have had little time for this Welsh beauty believing as she did that the Welsh, like the Scottish, do not 'travel well', I conclude that she and I do not have the same questionnaire and say so. As her tears flow piteously I take her form from her, see that it is the same as mine and the tear-stained question is 'Are you monogamous?' 'It is monogamous. Monogamous.' 'What is this moggy-moose?' Despairing of ever seeing Home again I look at her gorgeous, vacant face, her heaving bosom, and the way she holds her pen in her left hand awkwardly curled making writing a painful process to watch and patiently ask, 'Do you have a boyfriend?' 'Yes,' she answers rather doubtfully. The room is silent. No-one looks, everyone listens. 'Are you faithful to him?' She considers this carefully and then launches into a long story about last Saturday, alcohol and a memory lapse. I flick through her form. Her writing is illegible. She can best be described as illiterate. I choose to be softer, kinder. 'The answer to moggy-moose is sometimes'. I pick up my pen and fill it in for her. I risk elimination for this but I can no longer bear the heaving chest.

I never see her again after that day and assume she was taken away and shot.

I turn back to my own form with a heavy heart. I rush it. Some of my answers will come to haunt me in the next few months. Would I have sex with someone for money and if so how much? Easy. I opt for two pounds forty seven. This seems to me to be such a precise figure it implies due consideration and reverence for the system – that, or taking the piss. The choice is theirs. There is a disproportionate curiosity about my sex life and, given my age, much of it is ancient history so I make things up and forget people and events and generally fudge times, places and numbers. I am reluctant, too, to say much about my family or friends, feeling that I am the one volunteering for This Thing, whatever it is. I am more forthcoming about David and sum up our relationship by writing that, when a man of eighty plus says he will love you until the day he dies, it carries with it certain credibility. Not all my answers are lies and the truth, for what it is worth, is there for all to see.

I plough on. Having had a lifelong fascination with myself it is the questions about Me that most engage my thoughts. I do not, however, lose sight of Big Brother in all my narcissism. The facts, the intimate details of my life and the lives of those close to me, the truth, the half-truths, everything is one way. The flow is entirely from me to them. I don't know what will happen to this information, who will see it and how it will be used. And, despite my self-absorption or because of it, I guess I am less likely than most to experience a journey of self-discovery by taking part in a television game show however much its origins lie in a simple but ingenious social experiment. Put a group of disparate people in an enclosed space, set the fuse and see what happens. For my purposes at the moment I chose to suspend my discomfort and proceed. For now I am intrigued by their questions and what they tell me about Big Brother.

They are asking me to describe myself in three or four words like my mother [omni-competent, clever, angry] and my father [suave, clever, cruel]. This, too, is difficult. As I get older I find I know more and understand less. This includes an understanding of me, particularly in relation to the rest of the world. I believe this matters not a jot.

Someone recently gave me a biography of an American poet Edna Vincent Millay saying Millay reminded him of me. I cannot see it myself. I am aware that I am not always as sympathetic to the American view of things as I should be. I am too quick to laugh. Too quick to point out the risks of living in America or of being American. Only recently an American was telling me about the security necessary to ensure the safety of his President on a trip to China and was affronted when I pointed out that the number of American presidents who have been murdered in America at the hands of Americans far outnumbers those who have died in China or anywhere else at anyone's hands. This becomes a worry to me. I don't want Big Brother to eliminate me on the grounds of prejudice or to think me over-confrontational but I don't want to appear too floppy. The significant number of questions relating to one's use of violence and criminal record suggests that this little verbal bating might not matter to them too much weighed up against my shortage in the asbo and prison record department. I am looking a bit thin too on the drug scene being unable to confess to any usage and no real knowledge of what 'rehab' might mean. So when they ask me about people I don't like I settle for 'underachievers' which in any case pretty well covers Americans – except for jazz which is the only valuable thing America has given the world...that and George Clooney. I mention later that I dislike all music but while this may be considered unusual I judge it to be an advantage in a situation where there is none i.e. in the Big Brother house.

Back to Edna Millay for clues to my three allocated adjectives. Millay and I are alike, they say. A country-loving American poetess – her poems are embarrassing juvenile crap, by the way – with red hair and a penchant for drugs, alcohol and other people's husbands. I don't think so.

I toy with the innocuous little word 'kind'. The evidence is overwhelming. Witness my treatment of the Welsh heaving breasts. Into my mind comes a vision of the people in Portugal with whom we built up a relationship of sorts and who we miss – a gipsy family. These were not the picturesque painted caravan type but a mother and father, five boys all under twelve and a new baby girl – at last – struggling to survive the cold and wet Portuguese winter under a flimsy tent. Much of their charm lay in the long five miles between their home and our prestigious villa in the hills with its huge pool and bougainvillea- clad terraces. Moved by their plight I gather armfuls of woollens, blankets, a duvet and various odds and ends. With some trepidation, fearing causing offence or violence, we make a plan. We would take the boxes in the boot, David would keep his wallet hidden, the engine running and I would jump from the car and hand over the boxes and we would make a fast getaway. In the event we arrived at this dusty roadside site to find the family sitting by their smoky fire. They crowd round me, the mother hanging back a little, shyly.

'Do you perchance speak English?' Oh, for god's sake, Lesley. Now I'm Shakespeare. The eldest of the boys answers in perfect English, 'But of course!' It is a strange world in which we live and I understand less each day. Because the contents of the boot seem a little dull to me I have bought the children bags of sweets. The father takes them from me and say 'they are for later'. Perhaps he is mindful of their teeth, though looking at them it seems a bit late for that. There is much gratitude and handshaking and we feel truly ashamed of our apprehensions. As a final friendly gesture the smallest boy, about knee-high, picks up the hem of his vest, which is his sole garment, and waves his willy at us. As we drive off we wonder what they will make of the set of placemats with pictures of eighteenth century Bath including a picture of our previous house in the Royal

Crescent. Now does this show that I am kind or is it simply patronising? It's a fine line.

I think other people might describe me as fun. Certainly alligators think so. Proof of this came last year in Portugal when we ignored the advice of friends – 'You are just encouraging them in their cruelty to animals and they feed the lions on half-dead donkeys' – and go to the circus. Small, family owned circuses are a feature of Portuguese village life. One of my favourites featured a Chinaman on his water organ. Appropriately at the climax of the show we were plunged into darkness and he struck up a chord on his huge organ and as the music rose so, too, did coloured cascades of water drenching most of the fifteen people in the audience. It was much more impressive that son et lumiere in Karnak, and much funnier. Though, if I were being picky, I would have to say it was perhaps three quarters of an hour too long.

The first act was the lions and tigers. Though caged, they are within inches of their faces. Wonderful creatures in prime condition racing round and round. All those half dead donkeys, I suppose. Controlled by a buxom girl barely contained in a gold lame body suit. But she is totally in control, the child's plastic gun at her belt giving her confidence or the knowledge that compared with a half dead donkey she would represent little more than a snack. Acrobats. High wire act. No health and safety here. Clowns who engage David in their act. By the interval we are more than ready for a rest particularly as here everything starts at ten but runs late and it's already one in the morning. We buy coke and popcorn and a magic wand that changes colour when it works, which isn't often, and realise that six people who simply change costume man the whole show. The lion tamer looked far more fearsome when she sold us tickets and now sells hot dogs.

After the interval we are a little disappointed by the reptile act. At first. A man and his assistant, the lovely lion tamer, bring out box after box and disgorge snakes and crocodiles within feet of where we are sitting. Size it seems does not impress us. We are nearly as bored as the inert 12-foot alligator lying there before us.

Who can say what changed that? From being a sleeping hulk of taxidermists delight it opens one eye and looks straight at me. The other eye flies open; it is awake and running. And how it runs. The Portuguese family sitting next to me scatter leaving their granny to cling to my arm. But it's not her that interests the alligator. It is coming straight for me, its mouth slightly open and saliva running expectantly down its chin. By now it has its little feet on the wooden blocks that mark the ring and I can feel its breath on my face. The granny is screaming. The noise in the otherwise silent tent halts it in its intention and the alligator stops to think. The reptile 'trainer' has now flung himself on the alligators back and pulls it back from my face. A brief struggle ensues and all six circus family drag the alligator away. Granny is a sobbing lump of terror but her family have recovered and are hysterical with laughter. It is the end of the show. I have remained calm throughout fortified by the knowledge that I now have proof that at least in this unappreciative world alligators find me fun.

I think that I should describe myself as intelligent since I have described both my parents as being clever. I don't want anyone to think it has missed a generation. Anyway, if intelligence can be defined as the ability to put oneself in a favourable situation, then I am a genius. I want for nothing in life and I am much loved.

So in to the box to describe myself go – KIND, FUN, INTELLIGENT. I look round the room and see again how different I am from the other would-be contestants and pop down ECCENTRIC for good luck.

I have ploughed through the form. It is now a document packed with every piece of information about my past, my parents, my schooling, my sex life, my hobbies, things I love, things I hate, my taste in books, films, music, ambitions, achievements… The other applicants are still hunched over their paperwork so at least I have finished first. Competitive.

Despite my wide-ranging thoughts, I haven't actually been to too much trouble and wonder what will be made of my hurried answers. I think of Earl Spencer, a man for whom I carry no brief, who said 'Perhaps I am the terrible person the media says I am.' I have a glimpse of what he means. Perhaps this carefully, cleverly designed document does reveal the person I really am. Or not.

CHAPTER TWO

I have been told by those who know no better that I am spoilt. My general philosophy in life is that it is not necessarily true that one person getting what they want need be at the expense of someone else. Further I have found that if I get my own way then everyone around me benefits. It seems to me that it is a sign of intelligence to be 'spoilt' at 60. But that doesn't mean I haven't had disappointments.

We are driving up to and, as it turns out, round and round and round Birmingham for yet more auditioning. I have plenty of time to consider the forthcoming day and its potential for disappointment. I look across at David as he nobly drives me to the elusive venue. We have talked long and hard about the implications of my present venture but thanks to Big Brother's non-disclosure policy, we have no information on which to base any decision. Perhaps today will give us some answers.

I tell David he is being incredibly supportive in all this. 'You are being supportive or very clever. I can't decide which.' Not for the first time I pause to admire his distinguished face. Already having described him as a gentleman, I must remember to tell Big Brother he is handsome. I am relating everything to the Power that controls me. Supportive, or clever? 'Both,' he says, looking for all the world like a young Stewart Granger.

Then I remember Pamela Stephenson's hugely successful book about Billy Connolly. It seems that Billy is dismayed to find himself going grey. From the hair on his head to his pubic hair he is going grey. He bemoans that, in a certain light, his willy looks like Stewart Granger. So now, on top of all my other trials and tribulations, I suffer the disappointment of being married to Billy Connolly's willy.

I decide not to mention this as Big Brother has so far shown itself to be powerful and clever but not prone to outbursts of humour.

Why are we doing this? This battling through the torrential rain to some god-forsaken place? It's certainly not the money. We are so rich we can live out our days in luxury – so long as we die next Tuesday.

Perhaps I am in denial about my forthcoming birthday. My sixtieth. I am told it will bring huge benefits. A bus pass and free medicines. I scoff. I have never been on a bus in my life and don't intend to now and, equally, have no intention of being ill and requiring medicines. I see no benefits. I don't want to be one of those dreadful old wrinklies who wears sports gear and trainers and lipstick that bleeds and claim affinity with their teenage grandchildren and 'flirts' with young men. I can remember not so long ago when I was young and gorgeous and only kept a packet of smoked salmon and a bottle of champagne in the fridge. Will I soon have little bowls of indistinguishable bits of green covered in cling-film? Will I soon be looking at Marks and Spencer's clothes and saying they have improved out of all recognition – when we know they haven't – and 'man-made fabrics make such sense' Will I begin to reminisce about the 60's and say the Beatles made the best music when really I hated them then, and hate them now? Will I fuss about split infinitives? Will I be afraid of an unplanned cough or sneeze for fear of leakage?

Or will I, worst of all, audition for a television show specifically designed for twenty year olds?

The Birmingham audition is tedious and I am not performing at my best. Despite arriving promptly, unlike the other contestants who are infuriatingly casual about such matters, I am kept waiting for hours. Moved from corridor to corridor. Silently watched. Surrounded by the victims of the government's wicked care in the community policy. Shoved into another homemade cardboard room, a reject from a Blue Peter project and asked questions by invisible voices. They interrogate me on my long forgotten answers to their ruddy questionnaire. They ask, I answer and then long, maddening pauses. Why, they ask, did I put on the form that my ideal fantasy career would be as a royal corgi? Well, it seemed funny at the time and 60-year-old women are not famous for their fantasy careers. Why did I put Angela Burdett Coutts as my hero? They sound a bit peevish so perhaps there was a run on Angela that day in Cardiff. It was a lie. For years I have been in love with Kelly Hoppen, but I keep quiet about this as the person who put together these sheets of black paper and sticky back plastic into a makeshift studio like an inferior Acorn Antiques wouldn't know about the sainted interiors goddess. I put up a staunch case for Angela, Charles Dickens' wealthy female friend.

They turn their beady questioning to the Women's' Institute, of which I am a member. I tell them about the forthcoming programme in our area. We are looking forward to Christmas when Vida Gleed is coming to entertain us with her handbell ringers. Except there's a problem and Vida hasn't got any handbell ringers, just handbells and there is talk that the members will have to ring the bells under Vida's instructions. I have warned the Committee that I cannot always be relied upon to behave well in such circumstances. I sense that Big Brother is with me on this.

They want to know – obsessed as they are by the W.I. seeing it, perhaps, as a threat to the omnipotence of the Big Brother organisation – if I can make jam and scones. I explain patiently that David has said that he needs to make a household file before he dies with a map of the house with the kitchen outlined in red so I know where it is. They ask how David will cope with me being away.

I think of him now down in the foyer amongst life's flotsam and jetsam wearing his new overcoat, a vote for a future this, a brown lovat with a dark velvet collar. A cad's overcoat. Though these young persons masquerading as Big Brother wouldn't know what a cad was. A coat that only a man with supreme self-confidence could get away with, and I pine to be with him. Why doesn't your husband – disconcertingly they call him David – why doesn't he want to do this? The cameras and the tapes whirl capturing every idiotic thing I say. I explain that, although married and happily married, compatible even, we are completely different in most respects. He will not miss me domestically but, hopefully, will be devastated by my absence. I have a photograph of him with me that I offer to them or suggest that they might like to inspect him in person as he is downstairs. I haven't forgotten the all-seeing cameras but I know I am not performing well, in the sense that I am not amusing even myself, and could do with a bit of supportive company. I hear rustling and rumblings behind the screen and then lots of questions about my Royal Connections. So that's why they want me! I tell them that I am the one volunteering, not my friends, and they press and press and get nothing more from me so they can make it up if they chose. Which they or others will, no doubt.

We flee Birmingham with no more information than when we arrived. No surprises there then. Big Brother playing power games and me still intrigued.

Such disappointment! But nothing to compare with the evening when I was promised that I would fly. David Copperfield – not the David of Dickens fame but the American magician – is holding an evening of magic at Earls Court in London. We were promised that the highlight of the evening would be a display of flying. Mr Copperfield would select a person from the audience and, by use of magic, would enable them to fly. It was on this understanding that I parted with two hundred pounds for two tickets. In David's dreams he can fly but I feel that two hip replacements militate against flight and it is my turn. Hopeful as ever, convinced that I would be chosen I splashed out on a modern take on a World War 11 flying suit, an all-in-one affair with jaunty zips and pockets. We were aghast when we were shown to our seats. We must have been a mile from the stage and Mr Copperfield would indeed have needed magical eyesight even to spot me at that distance. For us to see him there were television screens dotted about the stadium, which isn't very helpful to me as I am one notch off needing a guide dog. In any case, curiously, David Copperfield chose instead a lycra-clad nymph in the front row whose name he already knew, as though by magic. A cynical person would say she could see the wires as Sharon flew through the air. At the end of the show we shuffled off despondently for drinks and found ourselves in an all night bar in the Earls Court Road. The evening brightened in the company of lovely and heavily pierced throng of colourful men who looked upon us kindly as one said, 'Look, Marky, heterosexuals!'

No promises – no information – no instructions – no warmth – no friendship from Big Brother. Such disappoint-ment. They have asked me why Big Brother is interested in me. I am beginning not to care but I say that I am different from The Others, an old fart from the Home Counties. From talking to the other contestants I hear that they see the prize to be won at the auditions is a Place In THE HOUSE. This is the ticket, the Willy Wonker ticket of all time, to fame and fortune. But, so the mantra goes in this new religion, the greatest and best of all these is CELEBRITY.

In Orwell's created world the state lottery prizes are imagi-nary. They really don't exist at all.

I have now truly entered a world of secrecy and codes. The further I get into the system the less I know. It is the opposite of any other organisation I have ever signed up to. There are three hour long telephone calls asking me the same old questions about myself and my life, over and over again. Checking what I have told them. Total strangers on the telephone using the daft code word, not giving me their real names, asking intimate questions, writing everything down in long-hand. I am extraor-dinarily generous, genial, and patient – and so, too, are my family and friends who, despite the cloak of secrecy, are being drawn into the game. I have been asked to give a list of referees who will be telephoned. This list is to include a lawyer, a police-man, a doctor and other professionals. I don't have to look far among my friends and family to find these. I wonder about the other contestants. I am told not to tell these referees that it is Big Brother, just an 'unimportant quiz show'. Anyway, in my world you might tell half-truths to nosy Big Brother but you tell the truth to your friends who, in any case, are not fools. Against Big Brother's instructions I warn my friends to expect a call. They wouldn't give out a piece of information otherwise. Each one phones immediately afterwards to report to me verbatim. 'So, you're going on Big Brother?' 'It's Big Brother, isn't it?' They know it is Big Brother because the caller goes to such pains to say it isn't and they know me well enough to know that if I am going on a naff television programme then it will be the biggest naffery of all time.

There are hour-long phone calls, one to Australia, one to Portugal, mainly focussing on my possible criminal record and propensity for violence. Perhaps David would be the more suit-able candidate. I have never hit anyone whereas he last hit a man in Arbroath in 1946 so is due to do it again about now. My friends are co-operative but a little fazed by the length and impertinence of the questioning. And perhaps they experience a tiny frisson of excitement at being involved in something outside our area of expertise and usual comfort zone. Fortu-nately they all come up with similar three words to describe me except for John, the lawyer, who says 'A celebrity who no-one knows,' which I like, but is 5 words but don't take him to court over it. Big Brother also phones David and quizzes him, again with an undue emphasis on violence. In the light of what follows he might have to revise his answer.

The relentlessly cheerful telephone voice of Big Brother tells me I have to send them a Police Check. It sounds so very simple.

Finding the police station in Tetbury isn't easy. It is hidden away and looks what it is – a sort of garden shed. The door was firmly locked. I looked for a notice of opening hours but all

there was was a large notice telling me it is my duty to personally arrest anyone smoking cannabis and, as far as I can tell
with my imperfect eyesight, anyone under 16. As though I
haven't enough to do.

I returned three times to the police shed before spotting a bell
labelled 'disabled'. It is clear to me that the disability is one of
height as it is set high into the wall and suitable for someone of
eleven feet tall. Despite having recently started stretching exercises in a sad attempt to get fit enough to mingle with Youth,
who I now see I must arrest, I cannot reach the bell. But I spot
a small pile of bricks nearby and judge that two or three of them
will give me an extra boost. I am not dressed for a building oper-
ation wearing as I am an Armani trouser suit and new red suede
gloves, judging this to be appropriate for meeting the police to
whom I am a stranger. But since I continue to conduct every day
of my life now on the assumption that I am being filmed and this
is a further test of my initiative, I prove that I have learnt something from my esteemed architect husband and construct a neat
little pyramid and I am able to reach the bell. Like a gazelle with
asthma I pounce down and start returning the bricks to their
proper place. Just then the door opens and the duty policeman
confronts me.

So there I am, an immaculately dressed older lady wielding
a brick outside a police station.

I am reminded of the Sainted Davina's words – 'you, too,
can be abused and humiliated on national television!' I had not
realised that this would happen on our own beloved doorstep.
The guardian of Tetbury's safety and security is an elderly
gentleman wearing a knitted cardigan. His incisive eye takes in
the scene and he ignores the brick and says, 'Have you come for
the cleaner's job?' Rather sharply I reply, 'I can see why you
didn't make detective.'

Inside the hut I explain what I need. A police check, please.
He could not be more amazed. He has never heard of such a
thing. 'What for?' I am quick here. 'For voluntary work with
vulnerable people.' Cunning and true.

He says that he will need to consult Cirencester and promises to contact me the next day. By now he is charming and deferential, which may be due in part to my having handed him my business card or a consciousness of the brick lying on the desk between us. The next day he telephones me and apologises profusely for mistaking me for a cleaning lady but says, gallantly, that he had mislaid his spectacles. Cirencester, too, it seems is crime free and has no need to prove it but a form is winging its way to me from somewhere more used to such shenanigans.

Peter Bazalgette, the Grande Fromage of Endomol, the Father of Big Brother, has spoken about the need for television to be culturally diverse and to exhibit a distinctive character. I think he would be proud of me.

I am anxious about the police investigation and what it might throw up. Only recently I was dashing through Grosvenor Square and paused to see what a dreadful mess the American embassy has made with its ugly bollards, barbed wire and security rubbish. Two heavily armed policemen approached me (except I think it is politically correct to call them police officers, just in case) and said, 'Good morning, madam.' 'Ah, so you recognise me, then?' I say. 'No, I don't think so. Should we?' I said I thought it outrageous that Americans should have such a gross building on our soil let alone be allowed to vandalise one of London's beautiful squares and that they might recognise me from a demo in the 70's when I was nearly arrested.' 'I was minus 10 then, madam.' Impressed but not giving an inch, 'I haven't time to argue this now as I'm late for luncheon at my Club.' I can see with hindsight this might have damaged my bid for Revolutionary Of The Year. 'Just as well,' he said with a smile belying the heavy weaponry.

When the police check arrives and they claim no knowledge of me I am relieved.

Later I am nearly a Victim rather than a Criminal when at one of the myriad London auditions a nasty looking young man with a surly manner, who claims to have a First Class

Honours Degree in Graphic Design from a Top British University, which is an oxymoron if ever I heard one, threatens to kill me, saying Big Brother could do nothing to stop him. I admit to being frightened by this but take comfort in the thought that everything is being filmed and he will have been caught on camera. To cover myself I do report this to one of the production team who agrees it is unacceptable but also agrees with me that it would be an imperfect crime, as it would be witnessed by five million people. So that's all right. Happily I never see him again. Liquidated I should think.

The auditions and London interviews now follow the same pattern: very short notice, dashes to London, no expenses paid, meetings on street corners with unknown and unlikely 'friends', taken to hotels, never told where, or who, given silly tasks to do, told again and again about secrecy 'no-one must know, or you will be out' and no-one answering why I am doing this, least of all myself.

Throughout the process it is my fellow contestants who give me the most cause for concern. They appear to have come out of a psychiatrist's manual. Every psychotic illness is paraded before me. I am surprised they can readily produce the documentation – driving licence, marriage certificates, birth certificate, bank card, two bank statements, doctor's details, two utility bills – that I have been told to bring to a meeting on a street corner in London. No other educated, middle class woman of any age in possession of her senses would do such a thing. In my defence, I took photocopies not originals but, standing outside myself looking on, I am amazed.

During the processes we are given forms to sign – forms that are presented to us hastily, there is no chance to properly read them. I ask for copies and am told 'there is no need.' I think they are about the rights to the filming of the auditions. On one occasion I see the girl next to me sign before reading and I say 'Shouldn't we read it?' and she shrugs and says there is no point and just signs and madly, rushed, so do I. Later I find that like Miss Moggy-Moose from Cardiff she can barely read or write.

Big Brother doesn't care. We are proles and proles are cannon fodder and don't count. I am more shocked in the auditions by the obvious instability and therefore vulnerability of some of the contestants. This may be resolved at the next audition because I am to see a psychiatrist.

As it turns out I see a psychiatrist and a psychologist. I am with each of them for over three hours. They have copious notes and test results from the myriad personality and intelligence tests that I have done over the months. I am uncertain if they are there to judge if I am too mad to appear on the show or not mad enough. In classic interrogation tradition they are quite different. One is smooth – evidenced by being the only person in the organisation to be wearing a tie – and the other is the absolute spit of Fitz, the Robbie Coltrane television police profiler. I do hope these interviews are recorded as the one with Fitz is especially funny. Fitz decided to play the 'I'm only a poor boy from the Gorbals born on a chip shop floor' routine to my 'because I'm from Gloucestershire I spend all my time eating canapés on a polo pony and talking to Royalty about Dickens.' They are both baffled as to why I wish to take part – so that makes three of us – and are full of unspecified but dire warnings. They deem me mad enough or not too mad to take part.

Both psycho-persons have been obsessed about 'secrets' and determined that he should be the one to expose my 'secret'. Indeed I feel that they would be so open to terrible disappointment I decide to come clean and break down and say I have been hiding something. They visibly cheer up. I tell them it is about my daughter and they grab pens and pads and settle in for a long, revealing session. Drawing it out a bit I finally break down and admit that she is a Consultant Psychiatrist as though this were the worst fate that could befall a daughter. 'Are you teasing me?' asks Smoothie, rather sadly.

The whole Big Brother experience has brought to light that, to my chagrin, I am pretty short on the secrets front. Probably because my modest misdemeanours have usually been caught out fairly promptly and would, in the face of the stiff competition of fellow better-qualified contestants, be deemed poor stuff. At one audition, in the late stages, we were asked to disclose a secret and then as a group place them in order of disgust. I was at odds with the group who thought very little of the contestant who confessed to having taken part in a vomiting game where the idea was to vomit in to someone else's mouth. The winner was the one who swallowed. I thought this high on my list of revolting secrets it not being one of the rituals of the Tetbury W.I. but was deemed 'too old to understand'.

I was shocked, too, by the barely suppressed anger of the contestants and the ready way they labelled, judged and condemned each other. All this so openly expressed surprised me coming as it did then so closely after the Shilpa Shetty and Jade Goody Celebrity Big Brother debacle, which might have been expected to make them at least more careful in what they said. I, naturally, was labelled 'too old' over and over again. That, it seemed to me, was the least of the differences.

It was from this audition that I returned to lovely Tetbury and felt as though I was walking dog poo on my shoe through the town and into my beautiful, innocent home. It is days before I am able to shake off the feeling of having been soiled.

Throughout all this I was the harbinger of a secret, one I kept from Big Brother, from other contestants and from the psychiatrists – no mean feat that I can tell you given all the checks and counter checks. One I have kept right up to this day. But reveal now.

David and I are the parents of two adopted children. Only yesterday, the day before the psychiatric grilling we have had to face that moment that all parents of adopted children must dread. The moment when the Big Questions are asked. That morning we had enjoyed a long stroll round the garden. The ritual is firmly established. We have breakfast. We do not encourage faddy eating. We are unsympathetic to guests who we have seen over recent years developing wheat, gluten, fat, starch, anything edible, fashionable allergies, preferring our visitors to be of the 'bring on the dead dog and trough of beans' variety. However, all four of us have different tastes first thing in the morning. Basile loves toast with lots of butter while Sinclair prefers something more savoury, and perhaps not surprisingly since they are both Portuguese, he likes bacalhau – cod - or a little flaked kipper served in warm milk. We are happy to indulge them. What is consistent is the table laid with linen and silver and a few flowers in a small vase – a tradition which I feel I should introduce into the Big Brother house.

It is a packed day. We are mindful of being Older Parents and so we over compensate, exhausting ourselves and them with walks and climbing, and gymnastics for Basile who is curiously skilled for one so chubby – Beth Tweddle is her hero – and football practice for Sinclair...and Sinclair helping Papa when Sinclair is adept at stacking logs, or painting a wall, and Boy Things...and Basile helping Mama with administration, though in her enthusiasm Basile tends to consign more to the waste bin than Mummy intended...and all doesn't go well as I hear David say those time-honoured parental words, 'Sinclair, I am so disappointed in you' and I gather there has been some unfortunate conjunction between football and vegetable patch...There are occasional accidents too, usually to Sinclair, being The Boy, who becomes over- excited and too ambitious. We don't want a repeat of the time we had to rush him to hospital after he had a fall and had limped in bravely suppressing his tears, and at the hospital we had to wait while a specialist was sent for and Sinclair's name was called and Our Little Hero tried to raise his feeble arm in answer but fell back in pain, and how after x-rays and examinations and painkillers and much passing of cash from us he was declared fit to be brought home and it was his first real experience of the car and he loved it all, except for the pain, and when home he lay on the sofa wrapped in a blanket and we fed him soup from a spoon and his sister looked on contemptuously. We remember, too, the time Sinclair went for a walk on his own and all the usual parental fears enveloped us and David lay exhausted from the search, unsuccessfully suppressing his tears, biting into the pillow sobbing, 'I loved that boy.' Note the past tense. And when he returned we grasped him to us, torn between anger and relief as we covered his unrepentant face with kisses.

We try not to worry about them when we go out and say we won't be long, just an hour or so at most, but always make the mistake of looking back at the house and there are their two little faces peeping though the curtains, waving their little hands and I am sure I can hear Basile crying into the wind, 'Write, Mama, write.'

That night when we are all snuggled together on the sofa I see a question forming in Basile. She looks across at her brother who pulls his father's dressing gown to him and sucks on its corner. She may well marvel, given how different they are in appearance and nature, and how different they are from both of us. I pull her close to me and begin to talk and Sinclair opens his eyes and he too is listening. I tell them the truth as David and I had agreed. I tell them how we had no intention of having more children, that our own families are complete and that we are too old in any case for more. I tell them about the wet and windy night when they as twins were brought to us quite unexpectedly, and while we had huge doubts at the time it was the best thing that ever happened to us, how when we looked into their tiny frightened faces, felt their vulnerability, how they clung together, defiant and brave, we had no choice but to say yes and let them into our hearts forever. And I told them about the cost and difficulty of bringing them to England with us. And of how, whatever we have given them and whatever we shall give them in the future, they have given us so much more in terms of love. And of how proud we are of them, now they have grown so big and strong and are generally so sensible.

We have discussed the implications of the Big Brother experience for Basile and Sinclair and agree that it is best to keep them well out of it. Above all we fear that publicity about them could result, as it does for the offspring of celebrities, in kidnapping attempts. However, mindful of the future attention of paparazzi, we decide that Basile should go on a diet. We can just see the magazine photograph now and its attendant headline – LESLEY'S FAT PUSSY AT THE WINDOW.

Chapter Three

Every day, in every way, Winston and I are coming closer together.

The psychologists have told me that nothing in my life will be the same again after Big Brother. I ask for specifics and they say it is likely that I will be spat on in the street. Street spitting is not a feature of Tetbury, though I do remember that there was talk of the Duchess of Cornwall, before she was the Duchess, having stale croissants thrown at her in Somerfield. I know this to be a lie as David often buys bread there and it is always wonderfully fresh. They are right, however, in their prediction that changes are afoot. I set changes in motion right back in January after the Cardiff audition.

Convinced that while Big Brother is undoubtedly secretive, power-mad and to date humourless, it is not stupid and will have seen the good sense in choosing me for the summer show I have been preparing myself for the challenge.

I see that one of the great problems ahead is the age difference between me and the other likely candidates. Although I have been shocked by their general listlessness at auditions I still feel that I am going to need personal stamina to face the rigours of long days in a confined space and what I hear are called 'tasks'. I look forward to the latter. I am highly competitive. Only recently I won the homemade Christmas cracker contest at the W.I. My success was only slightly tarnished by my friend Jackie's comment that the high vote for me was out of pity. I admit to being hopeless at such things but determined to win, I had thrown a great deal of cash at it, huge quantities of pink crepe paper, glitter and feathers and the end result was huge. Sticky, too. Looking at my two-foot long creation David remarked, with his critical designer's eye, that it was bit over the top. What cheek.

I also expect to have little sleep and a rather disrupted diet. An exercise programme is required. I enlist the aid of a personal trainer. Practising for celebrity already. I take Vanessa Feltz as a role model but plan for a greater weight loss, improved muscle tone and less of a twinkle in the eye. So, unlike her, I plump for a female trainer. Zoë is young, whippet-thin, toned and gorgeous. Despite this I like her.

Zoë has until June – I think it is June – to turn me in to a finely honed machine. I hope she does better than my previous regime in Portugal. In the interests of marital solidarity, or is that solidity, I joined David for his early morning exercises. These took place on the terrace by the pool. An idyllic setting amongst the hills above Faro with a view down to the sea. The sun shone and the smell of the lemon and orange blossom was intoxicating. A series of simple stretching movements – nothing too energetic since we are working on some ancient principle of gentle, unthreatening exercise of our own invention. We haven't bothered with Lycra as we feel this to be hot and unflattering and so we are nude. The sessions culminate in a simple exercise of our own invention.

We stand twelve feet apart from, but facing, each other. With arms raised and hands theatrically extended we run gently and gracefully towards each other. When we meet our tummies, being the most prominent of our features, bump. We then walk backwards and repeat the manoeuvre. Five or six times is the current record. Sadly it is mirth, not lack of motivation, that prevents us from doing more. The whole exercise owes much to the Royal Ballet – Darcy Bussell, eat your heart out – and Dawn French but with a touch, we guess, of the Teletubbies.

I trust that Zoë, with her university degree, professional qualifications and Territorial Army experience, will beat this and I confidently hand the problem over to her. I decide to tell her why I am doing this as I don't want her to think I am just an old granny poseur preparing for a session of bingo, however arduous I find that. We have to be 'focussed'. As a true professional she grasps the challenge and we see each other two or three times a week. For someone who is a control freak I find it remarkably easy to hand over control to someone who is good at what they do. Zoë has the good sense to know that I don't need or wish to know 'why?' I am a gift to artists and craftsmen because if I like them or their work I am happiest to commission them and give them free rein. I don't look at a piece of work and ask 'how?' For me the pleasure lies in the magic of not knowing.

So, Zoë, here's a fat, flabby body. Get on with it. And she does. We stretch and run and cycle and I balance on a large ball and even on my head, until I fall off, and she times me as I do interval running which is my favourite. That's where I run 100 yards and then walk 100 yards and then run again...I prove to be brilliant at the walking bit. Zoë is good, too, but a little more astute than I had hoped. When I break down and my lower lip wobbles and my eyes fill with tears she is merciless. Faux-crying, she calls it.

I declare to the world that I am on a diet. I only do this because I expect an outcry along the lines of 'you must be joking... thin as a reed...you are on the verge of anorexia as it is...' and I could happily drop the whole silly idea. But I was, as always, hoisted on my own petard. Rarely has so much enthusiasm been shown for someone else's suffering. I took the precaution before starting of undertaking a fattening-up programme. I lay for two weeks on a sofa being force-fed. For someone who loves food it sounds heavenly but I found that food, like sex, can be at its best when forbidden or scarce.

In any case our diet is already excellent. David, who supervises culinary and domestic matters in our household, was brought up in the Elizabeth David school of cookery. Our eating is decidedly Mediterranean in origin and concentrates on the best ingredients simply cooked. David himself is a brilliant cook. It is unlikely that we would be together otherwise. The two skills of architecture and cooking have much in common – a cup of this, a pinch of that, a bit of stirring, a slap it on and go for presentation sort of thing. I have never felt drawn to the idea of cooking. I see it beset with difficulties. Firstly I am by nature unable to follow instructions. Recipes always sound too officious to me so that if it says two ounces I suspect that four might be better. That is why David has requested that I do not make cheese straws again as after my first and last attempt he said, cruelly but truthfully, that they would be useful if we ever came to build an extension to the house. Secondly, I see the major pitfall awaiting the cook is that it is not a trick that can be done once. Do it well and you are expected to do it three times a day. Hence the cheese straws. I am a one-trick pony.

But it is a trick I have to learn.

The Big Brother programme may be dressed up as a social experiment with all sorts of psychobabble attending it. But essentially it's a game. And games need game plans. One of mine centres around Miss Moggy-Moose from Cardiff. I know that given the huge numbers who attend the auditions up and down the country and her 'cheating' in the written test, she is unlikely to be a Chosen One. However, she is possibly typical of the sort of girl who may be Chosen. Mindful that I am likely to be marginalized in the House by my great age, amongst other differences, I will need a small coterie of chums. The ability to rustle up a foodie treat would be a good weapon here. I picture the scene. A broken finger nail perhaps. A lost hair extension. Sobbing. Heaving chest. Auntie Lesley rushes to the rescue with a diverting offer of...perhaps not my brick-like cheese straws...an omelette!

I have never made an omelette in my life and assume, on the basis of the fuss people make about them, that they are terribly difficult. Just as the exercise has required a serious shopping trip for equipment – Juicy Lucy tracksuits, spotty trainers and the like – cooking an omelette takes me in to new shopping territory. I am in a new cook shop in Tetbury absolutely thrilled with its new consumer possibilities. I want everything but leave with a miniscule nutmeg grater, two fluorescent spatulas and a mug with George Orwell, Nineteen Eighty Four, inscribed on the side. Next I am in a kitchen design shop drawn to a ridiculously named 'Shaker' kitchen in pale cream. This could be an expensive omelette.

Cooking, I am learning, can be a slow business. I doubt I have the patience for it. Zoë, who is taking her job with me very seriously, has given me a bag of strange brown beans for my birthday. I hand them in at the door of the kitchen and more knowledgeable hands than mine soak them in water for three days and boil them for four. The outcome is a foul-smelling brown mess, which reminds me of something last seen in a lavatory pan and, given the taste, I suggest in future we cut out the middleman and just pop them down the loo. 'Lovely,' I tell Zoë, 'but I couldn't manage too many of them.'

David demonstrates omelette making. I chat away – mostly about my schooldays and how I dislike teachers and being taught – and I miss the finer points and we do end up eating rather a lot of omelettes. After serious warnings from David about the source of the eggs, the chickens, the cooking pan, the reggiani parmegianni or whatever, the butter, the heat of this, the room temperature of that, I feel terrified, as is probably the intention. It is a skill that I persevere with thinking it will come in useful if I can possibly master it. There are plans to teach me soup making and a simple but elegant shepherd's pie. At this rate I may have to defer my entry to the House until next year.

I am less confident about the usefulness to me in the House of one of David's other skills. Snobbishness. This is a subtle business. He recently set up a secret organisation called 'Snob World', the nature of which is by design a mystery to the outsider. I haven't been asked to join. In fact there are only two members – David, of course, and a Lady R. Lady R. is a grand, elderly lady as well as a Lady, the two things often being mutually exclusive, and is the President of Snob World. We met her at a musical concert. David and she bonded literally and instantly when she fell in the foyer and David gallantly managed to soften her fall by flinging himself between her and the unforgiving marble floor. I suspect it had been many years since the lady had mixed flesh with a man but she seemed not to find it entirely unpleasant. Later at the supper table people were speaking about David's varied and various talents. I felt I should take some reflected glory in this so said, 'I very wisely chose a husband who as well as other skills can cook.' Lady R. not to be outdone replied, 'I chose a man WITH a cook,' thus securing herself a joint founding membership of Snob World.

She knows nothing of this as David says it would be terribly vulgar to let her know and quite superfluous as he doesn't plan anything so plebeian as members, or meetings or newsletters.

I have been accused of snobbishness whatever that might mean. If a definition includes an undue respect and awe for those of perceived or imagined social superiority then I am entirely innocent. There's not a deferential bone in my body. Now, after all the running, jumping and eating brown beans, I can see all my bones.

Zoë has designed a modest training programme for me to take in to the House. This is supposing that Big Brother doesn't have Physical Jerks in mind. Knowing from the folklore learnt at auditions that paper and pen are not allowed I have to learn the programme. It is cunningly designed to be as unfunny as possible and unobtrusive as space will be limited.

Big Brother Training Programme

Mobilisation:
Roll shoulders forward and backwards
Neck to left and then right
Chin to chest [lengthen]
Full arm rotation – biceps brush ear
Hip circles – both ways – start small, gradually increase

Knee raises
Leg swings
Ankle rotations, flex and extension
Arms/shoulders:
Keep arms at shoulder height – tiny circles forward and back
Arm in front at shoulder height, tiny up and down movements
Slow movement down to 45 degrees, fast up to shoulder height
Same movement as previous but now plus one litre water bottle
1 litre water equals 1 kilo!
Bicep curls
Chest press and then a harder option which adds the tummy
Shoulder press
Oblique raise

My favourite is the oblique raise as it means the whole thing is over.

Do please note that Zoë has included the cunning and innovative use of a water bottle in the place of weights. Zoë is confident that there will be one readily available in the House. Personally I think we are all whistling in the dark. I am trying to learn the programme but fear of the whole adventure is numbing my brain. I persevere as I have been afraid of few people in my life – my mother, my sister, my daughter – and Zoë is beginning to creep on to the list. There are going to be millions of people watching me on television and it is Zoë I fear most. You can't be afraid of millions of people when you don't know them. Can you?

My final interview is in London. The atmosphere is heavy and the Big Guns have been brought out. By now over the months I have met, spoken to and seen dozens of the production team. Boys and girls rarely over 30. Like all the unsatisfactory candidates, the production staff are taken out on their 30th birthdays and liquidated. They are Peter Pan- like, dressed like children, the girls in smocks and floaty dresses and bracelets on elastic with love heart sweets, the boys in oversize but still skinny jeans. They are sweet and daft and sly and cunning all at the same time. There is a tension beneath the easy use of shortened Christian names. I don't ask them questions. I know there is no point. They will say they don't know which could be true or just a stock answer. Either way it makes me appear peevish which is not what I want. They concentrate on the tiny piece of the jigsaw that is their immediate job. Their common youth and the informality amongst them make it impossible for me to work out any pecking order. But I know at this interview, which turns out to be the very last, that the Big Cheeses have been gathered together and we are perilously close to the precipice of decision-making. Big Brother and I are keeping our cards close to our chests.

It strikes me as I sit there on a little chair in another card-board studio in a grotty hotel room with great lights shining into my eyes that the myriad procedures that I have been through are true to Orwell's original concept. That or some strange religious cult with all its' smiling young faces whose smiles don't quite reach the eyes. One phrase that is used strikes a sliver of ice deep into my psyche. FOR YOUR OWN GOOD. It has been said several times now and will be used increasingly in the next few weeks. It is not a phrase that sits well in the mind of a 60-year old woman – or certainly not in mine.

The Big Cheeses – the producers – are being Very Serious. In 'Nineteen Eighty Four' Big Brother is at once military and pedantic. So, too, is the style of these slightly older than the ranks official guardians of the biggest show on earth. Then comes what I am told all Big Brother aficionados know to be called THE TALK OF DOOM. Uniquely, I am given a copy of this document to take away, sign, and have signed by a relative or friend, like a child, and to return to be signed by the producer. They want no mistake here.

With an eye to Miss Moggy-Moose and her ilk, this document is read out, slowly, patiently, with great portent. The Ten Commandments would have been casually scattered to the wind by comparison. It warns of the negative consequences of taking part in the show – a death to all hopes of a media career or any job requiring credibility – the invasion of the media into one's personal life and that of one's family and friends – the uncovering of secrets...The producer elaborates. He says it is inevitable that someone will come forward with photographs or videos of me having sex. I marvel at our very different experiences. Because it is so clearly important to the team and the process I listen carefully and even demonstrate this by asking the occasional question but, because I can do two things at once, I think about the producer, not as a member of the Inner Circle of Big Brother but as a man. I can see that in other circumstances he is a man it would have been very easy to have fallen in love with and while he drones on I imagine a time twenty years ago when...and just in time I remember the Thought Police who can see inside your head and I pull myself together.

There is more talk about being spat at in the street and in all honesty I can't imagine why anyone would sign this form and go ahead with it. Yet from what I have seen of the other applicants I suspect they have short-term memories and selective hearing. 'You will not make money from this' becomes 'money'. 'You will not be famous or a celebrity' becomes 'celebrity, famous'. They know that from all 120 people or so who have entered the British Big Brother house over the years just a handful are remembered and not all those for good. They share a common arrogance. It won't happen to me, they think. I will be a star.

For me it is different. My ambition is not to be in Hello! magazine. Been there, done that. Well, in truth it was my house that was in Hello! We sold a house - that one we finally bought in Cornwall before deciding that we needed one closer to London and so plumped for Portugal instead - to Kate Winslet. Photographs appeared which included shots of the interior when we still owned it. The implication was that we had sold the house with contents or that the stylish furniture and paintings shown were the lovely Kate's. I spoke to the editor and he was so darned patronising I took the matter to the Press Complaints Commission and won. A rare victory. So Hello! won't be wanting me.

For me the Talk Of Doom covers old ground. David and I had this talk back in January. I am ahead of Big Brother or at least I think I am which is the name of the game for me. Their game is to have this little but vital document ready for later in case some disillusioned contestant claims to have been bamboozled and not told about spittle. Fair enough. The one thing I couldn't accuse Big Brother of is being encouraging. The producer, him of the steely eye and the tantalizingly nearly good looks, tells me that if I think this is all going to culminate in me sitting on television hosting a programme about Dickens then I should forget that straight away. No one will take me seriously ever again. I am surprised. Not by the vanishing prospect of a Dickens programme which has been done to death and had never crossed my mind but by his spite when he says it. The end of our affair then.

At this stage just a matter of a month before the launch of the show I still don't know if I have been selected. Indeed you don't know until the very last minute, until you step from the car on Opening Night. That date hasn't yet been published. But all our preparations in Tetbury are in place.

My family has been warned and briefed and are prepared. Mine is a small family, close and loving under a flippant, slightly cynical guise. We are generally warm and genial but capable of closing ranks and fighting to the death. My mother was a great admirer of the Spartans, especially their policy towards new babies, and that is how we are. Except not about our own babies. They are worried for me, apprehensive, but confident I can do this thing – whatever it is. I am less confident about myself but I am better informed that they are. Both about the programme and about myself.

We buy a paper shredder in case the paparazzi steal our gas bill from the rubbish, as we are told they most certainly will, and the first thing David test-shreds is its instructions. My bank is alerted and I set up complex financial arrangements that should see me out. I check my standing orders as though I were to be away for years. I am a responsible person with serious responsibilities.

Examples. Some years ago we spent the New Year in Sidmouth in South Devon and in that desperate mood that infects us on the dead first day of the new year we trawled the desolate and frozen countryside for entertainment. The previous year in Portugal I had been invited to a Foam Party – 'clothes optional' – but we declined on David's grounds that my spectacles might get steamed up and I wouldn't be able to see, which I thought would be a benefit. Anyway in Devon we found a donkey sanctuary. I have never seen a happy donkey. They have all forgotten the Jesus riding one story and have developed the ability to turn themselves into victims whatever the circumstances. A bit like the cast of Eastenders. There we are David and I having eaten too well for three weeks wrapped up to the eyeballs standing on a Devon hillside in the snow looking at a couple of hundred of the most miserable donkeys dreaming, presumably, of being ill-treated but warm in Spain. The lady in the education centre, a thinly disguised begging bowl of a place, and why not, suggested that we might like to make a financial contribution. I agree to a one-off donation and a modest standing order. Cunningly eyeing my new red coat the lady suggests that I might like to buy one of the donkeys a coat. I cannot help but agree. I consider the sum I paid for my coat and write them a cheque for a similar amount. Whether the sanctuary staff went to Jaeger for a garment I am not sure. I check that the standing order is in place for what could be a very long summer.

I also check the standing order for Kevin who is living the life of Riley at my expense in Australia. I met Kevin when I visited my daughter who lives there. On the way back from our tearful reunion at the airport she said there were one or two things we needed to do on the way back to her house. Time and twenty four hours in an aeroplane had dimmed my memory of her so I envisaged a stop at a supermarket for fresh milk or the like.

The stops included a bungee jump – only possible after the anaesthetic of a long distance flight during which I had lost the will to live somewhere over Singapore – and a visit to a koala sanctuary. You may well think as I did that koalas are sweet little creatures with a high ooh aah factor. Forget it. They are deeply unpleasant. Clingy, smelly, flea-ridden and ungrateful. Just having lost the contents of my stomach and my eyeballs as I jerked on a bit of string over a ravine I was in no mood to argue as an orphan koala was thrust into my arms. I was assured that if I made a financial contribution to his upkeep I could name him. It is some reflection of my mood at the time that I chose to call him Kevin. The Australians, however, were delighted as in one of those strange twists of culture Kevin is a 'posh' name in Australia.

I duly set up a standing order for Kevin which, in my terrible state, I miscalculated the exchange rate and each month from that date I send Kevin enough money to be educated at Goolagong for the rest of his life. In return I receive well-typed letters signed 'Kevin' each year on his birthday updating me on his news. David is sceptical. He does not believe that Kevin can write. The bloody thing better be able to write given the money I send.

All my over-elaborate plans and checking and counter-checking is my attempt to fool myself into believing that I, not Big Brother, am in control of the situation. But, hey, let's go shopping...

Despite what Big Producer reads from the Talk of Doom there must be an upside. I shall shop for this adventure. Along with everything else I haven't been told I have no idea what to take into the House, no guidance at all. Added to which I have just been told that if I am selected – big IF, they say – I will be called two days and two weeks before the start date, which still hasn't been announced and is giving rise to much public speculation, told to pack my cases and will be taken away from home to be kept in isolation until the actual date.

While those who follow the show know this it comes as a complete shock to me.

Worse than the thought of the Unknown House is the idea of some grotty holiday destination in the company of a smiling

Peter Pan religious convert. I ask for reasons and am told that I must be hidden from the tabloids and paparazzi. I explain that the best place to hide me is going about my business as usual in Tetbury. There is already some unease among my friends who can't understand why we are being so slow to reply to invitations issued for the summer months. This attitude won't do. Big Brother is short with me. Big Brother does not negotiate. Big Brother wants everything to be 'a level playing field'. Whilst being a liberal socialist I have never subscribed to the concept of level playing fields for myself. As soon as the start date is announced the baying press, they say, will be scouring the streets of Tetbury looking for potential housemates. I explain that my absence will make me more noticeable than my presence. Again, 'IT'S FOR YOUR OWN GOOD.' Then, priceless this, from a producer, 'we need to wean you off David.' So there's someone who has never had a quality relationship.

I set out on a shopping trip which could be a nightmare. One look at me will tell you that I am not a woman given to an excess of preening but three months of toiletries is some bag full. I go to Boots. I have developed a paranoia about Big Brother which extends to the thought that what I buy may well be stolen from me. I don't buy my favourite goodies instead go for cheap and simple. Three of everything, toothpaste, shampoo, conditioner, with careful self-rationing should see me through. I don't want them to be luxurious, as the less I love them the easier it will be to bear their loss. If they go, they go.

All I know is that I am allowed to take one suitcase and one overnight bag. I decide to sub-divide the clothes into two cases mentally. There will be one set for the so-called 'holiday' – I can't tell you the resentment I have built up about this – and the clothes for the house. The only Big Brother show I have seen is the Celebrity one with Ken Russell, Jade Goody and Shilpa Shetty. Difficult to know which of these to take as a sartorial role model! I think about what image Big Brother would want from me. Everything they ask indicates that it is the Gloucestershire W.I. country-loving academic

fart that appeals to them. I will go with that. As though there
were any other option open to me. I want to keep it simple
and easy. Staying 'crisp' is going to be difficult in trying circumstances. I shall spend one day and one day only attempt-
ing to resolve the problem.

I grit my teeth. Unlike my sister I am not a great shopper. She
is a true professional with an encyclopaedic knowledge of
goods, their location and comparative prices. We are very
different people. To Big Brother – she supplied one of my references, not because she was my sister, but because she was
deemed a professional having retired in the last few years as a
Director in the National Audit Office, an important functionary
that the media folk won't know, but should – she said that the
difference between us is that I am one of life's sprinters and she
is a long distance runner. It is certainly true that she would be
better suited to this game-show business than I am. For a start
she has a memory of her childhood whereas I have none of mine.
Before she was born when I was nearly seven – or was it six, you
see I can't remember - my dear Aunt Vera took me to Sadler's
Wells to see some swans dying. She asked if I had the choice
which would I prefer, to be a ballerina or have a little sister. The
words 'rock' and 'hard place' come to mind. I wanted neither.
Half a century later having given up any ambition to be a ballerina I am free to enjoy my relationship with my sister. Although
generally disapproving of my present adventure on the grounds
of my 'vulnerability', which I interpret as sisterly jealousy, she,
like the rest of my family, has taken the view that having come
thus far I might as well see it through. Which is her attitude to
shopping. She has more bed linen than John Lewis.

I could do with her help now. I can buy houses, properties,
businesses and cars but my track record with clothes shopping
is a sad story. In this, as in most other things in my life, I am an
unwitting victim.

Back to Portugal again. We are in San Bras, an unattrac-
tive town away from the tourist strip in the Algarve. Its only
claim to fame lies in the fact that the late Richard Whitely of

Countdown fame named it as his favourite holiday destination in the whole world. But then he was from Yorkshire.

We were at the local peasant market on a Saturday morning browsing through the undesirable goods on offer. Some huge brassieres caught my eye, enormous great constructions each the size of a dustbin lid and in remarkable beige elastic. Seeing that David was moving ahead to a saucepan stall, which would hold no interest for me, I stopped and idly fingered one of these impressive garments. The man behind the stall was typically Portuguese in stature. 'Your sort,' David calls them. No higher than my shoulder, unshaven, grubby and with a twinkle in his eye. My sort, indeed! It wasn't long after moving to Portugal that I realized that it is the only country in the world where I am admired by local men. Though I was quite popular in Malta.

In Portugal I am a magnet. One day we went with the local garden club high into the hills to look at the autumn wild flowers. We trekked for an hour deep into the country and admired a carpet of rare wild orchids. No one in sight except our odd little party of English gardeners. But, of course, it happened. Out from the bushes sprang one of the little men. He pushed aside the others in our group and lunged for me. Grazing my face with a stubbly kiss, he executed a wild leprechaun dance and then hopped and skipped up the road.

It happens everywhere. So it was in the market. The brassiere man is twinkling at me. I have done nothing to encourage him. Even keeping my eyes lowered – they are blue and much remarked upon in the land of the brown-eyed people. He holds up a pair of gigantic knickers and when he tells me the price I have to agree that given the quantity if not the quality of the fabric they are indeed truly value for money. Then he turns to his white van parked close by and, offering the ultimate sales come-on, says in English with a strong New York accent, 'Come into my van and try them on.'

I look round for David and see him engrossed in colanders. Why can I not form the word 'no.' No, Big Brother. A simple, firm negative will close the matter whether it be about white vans or reality television. Instead I mumble, 'I am with my husband,' as though under any other circumstances I would be in the back of his van knickerless. Is it this pliability that attracts Big Brother to me? I am a wimp. He looks around for my husband, locates him, is not impressed, shrugs and says, 'He is no matter.' I look at the grubby white van and turn and run and run. I report my near miss to David. His attitude is non-supportive.' If you had tried them on he might have given you a price reduction.'

Coming fast on the heels of an incident at the Max Mara shop in Quinta Shopping, that enclave of the wealthy European golfers and footballers wives, wegs and wags, I have every reason to be a nervous shopper. On a model is a deceptively simple dress. The sort of dress that should be taken to court for gross deception. A simple concoction of beige silk, draped and elegant. It would have looked wonderful on Grace Kelly or Audrey Hepburn. I never learn from my mistakes. I ask the stick-thin assistant if they have it in a huge size. She looks down at my feet and studies them. I hadn't thought to wear it on my feel but conclude it's a bit like childbirth when they keep asking you your shoe size. I am confident. My feet, if no other part of me, are small and in an attempt to look smaller still I have adopted the fifth ballet position. I read about this in a magazine. 'How to look a stone lighter without having lost weight.' All is well until I try to move and somehow my legs get entwined and I do indeed appear to be thinner – but drunk. The assistant brings forward a ton of beige silk and I know it is a colour that suits no one except Coco Chanel, and she's dead, but I'm in the cubicle and it's too late to go back.

It is then that I realize that this is a frock for which a degree in engineering is required. It has hidden zips, buttons, fastenings and drapings. By now it is firmly over my head and it takes a grip on my throat. I cannot breath. I call piteously for help. I am going to die in the Max Mara changing room and the only comfort I have is that I have my knickers on. David has, meanwhile, been

perched on a spiky little chair, placed there by a dubious assistant. He loves shops. Not the shopping or the merchandise but
the shop itself. He wants to examine every fitting and fixture
especially those behind the scenes. While I have just seconds to
live he is checking the mini-kitchen in the staff area. My cries fall
on deaf ears. Except for one lovely fellow customer who comes
to the cubicle and pulls at the garment. 'Get scissors and cut me
free,' I beg. Probably my last words, ever. I am prepared to buy
the garment in exchange for my life. My head is dragged from
my body but at last I am free.

I recognize my saviour as Lisa Tarbuck, now more famous
than her famous father. This does not make me feel better. This
woman has gone to the Algarve to get away from drama, but
at least she is laughing. Still panting I drag on my crumpled and
soiled clothes – there is no chair or hook in the cubicle and in
the melee they have been trampled – and hand the sweat-
drenched beige marquee to a bewildered assistant. 'No, I don't
think I'll take it,' I say and grab David and run from the store.

Thus I approach my day of shopping for the Big Brother
House with justifiable trepidation.

I have settled on a black and white theme. I guess there will
be enough other people going in to the House looking gaudy
and nude from their two week stay in Ibiza, or wherever. And
young. I aim to look like the sort of mother or grandmother
who is smart-enough-but-not-trying-too-hard-and-wouldn't-
let-you-down-except-she-upsets-the-apple-cart-by-going-on-
Big-Brother sort of way.

It is easier than I thought. I go to Harvey Nichols and French
Sole and Marks and Spencer and Thomas Pink and its all done
in a day and that includes lunch in the 3rd Floor Restaurant and
a glass or two of champagne to keep me going in what I swear
is still the best pick-up bar in London. So I am all packed,
everything neatly folded and wrapped in pink tissue and I am
ready to go. If I go. If I am chosen.

Now Big Brother wants to do a house inspection. Or, as they
put it, spend a day with me, following me about, learning more

about my life. I despair. There simply can't be more to know about me. They want to come here the next day. Bugger. I had planned to spend the day with Peter Ackroyd. Well not exactly **with** Peter Ackroyd but with his book about Turner. Having exhausted and been exhausted by Trollope, though I have formed a modest regard for him, I have moved on to John Ruskin against whom I have built up a satisfying personal hatred. I was really looking forward to it, but can see that it wouldn't make for exciting television. It's all a lie, this television game; my real life is about a day with Ackroyd and Ruskin. But I'm here to play their game not mine and so I arrange a lunch party for friends at a charming Tetbury hotel. She can see over the house, meet David briefly – he is very busy and not afraid to let her know that this is not his priority – have a decent lunch with some jolly people and I shall fill the day with a trip to the gym to meet Zoë, my trainer. This is not enough. She wants to stay for the evening and go 'clubbing'. The club scene in Tetbury is limited and we have just missed the W.I. meeting which I would die rather than take her to.

There is much discussion on her part about her 'cover' story. Much too much in my opinion. She settles for the idea that she should be a friend of my son. I do not. I haven't seen this girl but am unwilling to land my son with what I guess would be an unlikely if imaginary friendship. I cannot adequately explain this to her as I know by now that my world and the world of television producers have little in common, and they find it impossible to believe, knowing so little about the code which governs the world of the true professional, that my friends are perfectly capable of keeping a secret and would not dream of rushing off to report to the press. I tell my friends who she is, give the Christian name she has given me which may or may not be true, and tell them about the reason for the visit. When in doubt fall back on the truth, is my new motto.

Never before have I opened one of my homes to someone without knowing their full name, address and telephone number. I collect her from the station in a seething rage but she is charming, as they all are, and, soothed, I become a character from the Archers driving her round our glorious countryside showing off the brilliant mustard oil seed rape, explaining it to her and generally coming over all countrified. She looks over this house and there is a worrying moment when I offer her a drink. She has followed me through to the kitchen which is alien territory to me. In an attempt to find the cups and saucers I open a cupboard and, seeing saucepans or whatever, have to pass it off by chatting loudly about something else. I am opening cupboards in an increasing panic. I think I get away with it, or she thinks this isn't my house. Later, we have a jolly, alcohol fuelled luncheon. Although it breaks the 'rules' I think she is relieved that I have spilt the beans. We all comment upon her frequent loo visits. She is either slightly incontinent or has to change the batteries on her concealed recorder. We agree it's a rum do. I take her to meet Zoë and inspect the gym but refuse her request to ride out. You can't just hand over a horse to someone who hasn't ridden since she was six and say 'go get 'em'. I wonder if we have all 'passed' this test.

I am especially mindful during these last weeks of my responsibility to the W.I. They have been very welcoming to me since my arrival here in September last year and I have recently been asked to stand in for the President at a meeting during her absence. Last year there was a great kerfuffle when the Duchess of Cornwall joined our group. Media interest then was intrusive but our thirty-five or so ladies are made of sturdy and sensible stuff. I just wonder how, given the repeated warnings I have had from Big Brother, how they are going to cope again with this potentially even sillier situation. I have no idea, either, how I am going to be presented by the television programme, what from the extensive material/evidence they have about me they will select and how they will use or misuse it. I am a recent member of the W.I., a newcomer, and I have reason to have special respect for the organisation.

It was the W.I. who taught me a stern lesson about not being patronising.

Some years ago I was on the speakers list. At the time, in retirement after a career as a headhunter, I ran a small, but often successful service introducing people with a view to personal relationships, a happy marriage being the ideal outcome. The transferring of the professional skills of headhunting from the workplace to private lives gave the source of an interesting talk, or so I hope. One January evening in terrible weather I drove deep into the countryside and gave such a talk to a group of ladies.

Let me say now that if Jennifer Saunders had been to more W.I. groups she would have written a funnier series on them than Jam and Jerusalem. The world would have been surprised by the sheer variety in the membership.

This particular group had a significant young membership and the first question after the talk was about same-sex partnerships. Afterwards I was asked to judge the competition. This was 'a seasonal vase of flowers'. A tall order at this frosty time of year. One was outstanding. A magnificent display featuring orchids showing that the owner possessed a hothouse. In contrast there was a small glass pot, previously used for sardine and tomato paste spread, containing two very sad snowdrops. Eschewing the gorgeous orchids I pointed to the paste spread occupants and named them first, and the orchids second. There was a barely concealed outrage at this injustice but I held my ground, saying I felt the paste jar more accurately captured the mood of the season. The Chairman announced the winner and said that it was traditional for the speaker to be given the prize-winning entry. I looked across wistfully at the orchids. That will teach you to be patronising, Lesley.

I write to the local President and the Secretary of the W.I. to warn them in advance that I might be on a television show and to apologise in advance for any flak that might ensue.

As well as my local interests we now have David's position here to consider. In May he was elected to the Tetbury Town Council. We wonder quite how the town would take to the wife of one of its representatives being a Big Brother 'celebrity'.

I am all packed and ready. Nothing left to chance at this end.

Have I passed the house inspection? I don't know. The Big Brother spy wouldn't say anything. Despite my friend Faith's Gestapo-like interrogation she claimed not to know when the show would start. It's difficult to arrange anything for the summer not knowing if and when. But the hardest part for a controlled, controlling person is being controlled.

Worse is yet to come.

CHAPTER FOUR

In the world of 'Nineteen Eighty Four' it is almost impossible to travel freely out of London. Passports and documentation are constantly checked and rechecked and, while you are out of the reach of telescreens, Big Brother is still watching, watching.

It is now two weeks before the possible launch of the show. It is midnight and I am sitting in a car at the empty car park near the entrance to the Channel Tunnel. I am thirsty, hungry, exhausted and increasingly concerned.

The previous day I had been telephoned by Big Brother and told to go to Paddington station with my luggage. Not that I had been Chosen, but I wasn't Not Chosen. David and I said our goodbyes not knowing if I would be gone for a few days or three and a half months. There's a big difference, especially when you are 82. We knew that, according to Big Brother's self-appointed rules, we would not speak again or have contact of any sort until Big Brother said so. It could be nearly four months before we spoke again. Who could guess what our lives would be like then? On the station platform we re-enacted Brief Encounter without the steam and the grit in the eye. We were brave but both broke down minutes later, him by the side of the road on the way home and me in the crowded railway carriage. What if I had turned to the commuters, the city types, the lawyers and accountants and sales people, and said, 'I'm sobbing silently into my handkerchief because I'm going on Big Brother'? They would have turned back to their newspapers and laptops thinking, rightly, that I was mad.

At Paddington I'm not met as promised. As usual, hanging about in true Big Brother style for hours and hours, met at last by a Miss Selfridges-dressed production team clone, nice enough, who drives me through London and a journey that should take thirty minutes takes three and a half hours, because she doesn't know the way and I can't help because I mustn't know where I am going.

Another miserable room in another grotty hotel. Shut in the room with the girl who appears to know even less than I do, which is nothing, and I'm brought out every hour or so to go to another room for filming and questioning and written tests. I am dressed for travelling – to Ibiza, who knows? – and I'm in front of cameras, posing, going over the same old questions. Then I'm stuffing marshmallows into my mouth without swallowing 'in the style of a famous person'. I choose Maggie Smith and I don't think these people know who she is. The room has little pyramids of tissues and I ask about them and they say that previous people have been sick. Then a session in front of the camera with the psychology lot. More questions and a test to see what my body language tells about me when I lie. I have to say when and the circumstances in which I lost my virginity, once with the truth and the other a lie. The question is impertinent and I AM NOT ANSWERABLE TO THESE PEOPLE so in both cases I lie but, despite being so tired, I am inventive and wish they were both true.

It is eight at night. I guess it is dark outside but the curtains are firmly shut for fear of long distance paparazzi cameras. This is not a joke. Apart from the odd marshmallow that I may have inadvertently swallowed I have had nothing to eat or drink all day and, worst of all for me, I can get no answers as to what is happening next. I should know better than to ask. I guess the photographs and filming will be used on the programme and the spin-off shows and, in spite of my casual off-hand manner, it really is important to me. I look crap.

I am a real professional. I turn it on for the cameras and give them the best I can, as quickly as I can. I am furious with myself for being so entertaining and so lovely to everyone. The only giveaway about how I feel, and only I know this, is that for the very first time in my life I have started to swear.

And then suddenly I explode. It is late. I have my eye on Ibiza and an I.Q. test is shoved at me. I am matching squares and triangles and having to be creative and state the capital of Venezuela and it all becomes too much for me and I start screaming and swearing. That should give the ruddy psychologists something to get their teeth in to. Mrs Control has lost it. In true Elizabeth Jane Bott style I scream that I must see the Producers, not the Smiley One but the Unsmiley Ones, and they come to the room. With an imperious wave of the hand they clear the room and the three of us are alone together.

My main panic all week has centred around the fear of being cut off from my family. Australian Big Brother is being shown at that moment and our newspapers are full of articles about the death of the father of one of the contestants while she is in the house, and she is not notified. I have pressed this over and over again until I have said there must be an undertaking that I will be notified in the event of various specified problems at home. This is a deal breaker. I was told that I would have this opportunity before going in to the House. This would be too late for my comfort and I would already have been long out of touch with my family. Finally, late that previous day, I have written that I can only proceed on the basis that if during my time in the House my husband, my son, or my sister, who are all responsible, reasonable professionals, contact the back-up team and say I must be got out, then out I am. Despite my best efforts this is the best I can do. I take comfort in the thought that my family, individually and collectively, is a formidable force.

Underlying this very natural fear is a basic lack of trust. True, everyone is pleasant to me, charming even in some cases, but I don't know this organisation or its individuals. Beyond the thought that their business, and common sense, would determine that they don't want a very public fiasco – and even that I am uncertain of – I know they are working in their own best interests, not mine. IT IS FOR YOUR OWN GOOD is IT'S FOR OUR OWN GOOD in my mind.

The cracking point now, in this grubby enclosed hotel room in Docklands centres around a contract. Late last night after increased pressure from me, they sent me a fax of hundreds of pages, which constitute the contract between me and the production company. It is straightforward. In a nutshell I hand over my immediate life to them without question and they have control and I have no rights. I have been told I can consult a lawyer. It is 8.30 on a Saturday night, I am off to the gods alone know where tonight, probably abroad, and the only contact anywhere is through the production company's mobile phone which has demonstrated on the route to Docklands that great talent of mobiles of cutting out, going dead and generally being non-cooperative.

The Big Cheeses and I talk, and for me it is simply a relief to be away from the myriad Boys and Girls and their 'important' trivia. They do not coerce me and are discouraging. A clever ploy. The decision to go ahead is mine.

Which leads me to being alone that night or early morning at the Channel Tunnel. We are going nowhere as The Girl who they call my 'chaperone' – good god, I am a sixty year old woman not a Jane Austen heroine - doesn't have her passport. She has forgotten or lost her passport.

She has locked the car. On the journey down when we avoid motorways as that, they say, is the hideout of the paparazzi, I am escorted to the loo. There is a fear I will escape, or, worse, read newspaper headlines or, worse still, tell someone I am short -listed for Big Brother, or, worst of all, breath unaided. I crane my neck to catch a glimpse of the Channel.

I consider my position. I think I am in a state of shock but the very act of thinking means I am not. This is the moment when I have to put aside my doubts and press ahead. This has ceased to be an intellectual dialogue with myself, if it ever was. I have to accept that these are strangers that I have no reason to trust, indeed have good reason to distrust. However I do trust myself. Whatever faces me now I know I am alone and I know, too, that I am the best person to look after myself. I cannot ignore my fears but I can press on regardless of them.

Or I can throw myself in the Channel. This is an option I consider. There has been a slightly watery theme to the day what with tears on the train, sobbing over the marshmallow and unexplained questions about my ability to swim. 'Can you swim?' Three times.

Some deep instinct of foreboding made me say 'No. I cannot swim.' I said it firmly to brook no discussion. To settle the matter I have not packed a swimsuit, although I know The House is likely to have a pool of sorts. I am delegating pool parties to The Others. The truth, however, is more complicated.

Until last year I had never been able to swim. I was brought up in London and we were too poor to have our own pool and too posh to go to public pools. A huge and lovely pool in Portugal was the spur to put this right. This and my generous bid at a charity auction. The prize was the services of A Man who promised to teach the bidder to swim. A perfect opportunity but one which, as is customary with me, required extensive preparation. I sat in our darkened utility room with the tap running and with a peg on my nose for ten minutes at a time practising breathing techniques. I shaved my legs three times a day to aid aqua dynamics which has given them a grazed and shiny look. I also shaved other parts in preparation for snug swimsuit wearing. If it were Christmas it would be dangerous as I look like a turkey.

I also look up swimming on the Internet. I have to say I shall never be a compulsive surfer, of sea or web. Having access to all the information ever known to man has confirmed me in my belief that it is not what you know but what you do with it that counts. But I thought I might glean some handy hints ahead of my lesson. Research is everything.

Dwarf swimmers, it seems, sometimes have trouble balancing in the water especially when learning to swim. This is unhelpful. Indeed I can't judge how relevant this is to my situation. I am short, which is true. But dwarfish? Other advice confirms my long-held view that non-swimmers seldom drown since they have the good sense to keep away from water.

I am now crammed into my swim suit which appears to have shrunk despite never have been in water and I wait for The Man. No-one has awaited their executioner with more foreboding. I had hoped for bad weather. Let this be the one day in August that it rains in Portugal. A minor accident to The Man perhaps. Or me. Or David. Or anyone. Some technical problem with the pool. It is not unusual to hear of badly constructed pools that have split in half, come apart right down the middle sending debris and water cascading down the hill. Come on, gods, prove yourselves and save me.

At precisely the appointed time The Man comes up the drive on his gleaming motorbike. He is glossy and even from a distance I can see he is Keen. He exudes that most worrying symptom of which I can never be accused. Enthusiasm. We chat on the terrace and have a drink. All is going well and I begin to think that I have just paid for a talk on swimming and he will go away. He asks when I first developed my water phobia, as he calls it. I feel, if it were possible, even more inadequate. I can't elevate my feelings that seem entirely rational – as is my attitude to Big Brother – to the status of phobia. I just don't want to drown. I struggle to invent something dramatic but fall back on childhood memories of the freezing Kent coast and my mother's certain knowledge that swimming pools are full of pee, corn plasters and worse. David leaps in to help. He tells The Man that I must learn to swim as David's bronze life-saving badge gained some 63 years ago cannot be relied upon as, being bronze, it will only guarantee saving one person in three.

I have to take out my contact lenses and so am now blind. I have also lost the will to live.

The Man is enthusiastic about the water which is warm and chemical free. We talk about the benefits of a salt pool which this is and generally put off the fatal moment with chat. I had imagined the lesson would start with some jolly bobbing about clinging to the edge, some gentle jumping up and down to the sounds of encouragement from a Joyce Grenfell teacher. Far from it, 'You go down and lie on the bottom of the pool,' he says, 'and I hold you down with my foot, then let go and you will float to the top. With your eyes open.'

The Man is mad. I look round for support. David will rush forward, punch The Man, drag me out aided by bronze medal, and beg my forgiveness. David has gone indoors. Judas. Pontius Pilate.

I have never met The Man before. He says he has a certificate. I have not seen it. For all I know he could be a mass murderer who specialises in killing people in their own pools.

Here the parallel between my swimming lessons and the Big Brother experience is obvious.

The next thing I know I am at the bottom of the pool with The Man's foot on my back with my eyes open. I am amenable to a fault.

Within half an hour I am thrashing about and The Man says, 'You are swimming.' I have swum a width. Albeit underwater. Face down. Eyes open. But I am swimming. The Man asks if I am aware of what I have been doing with my legs. I cannot speak being full of salt water. 'You must have been a frog in a previous life,' he says. This is not flattering but well meant. The Man calls to David to see the miracle. David is suitably impressed and makes all the right noises. Having done it once I think I shall never have to do it again. But it is like cooking, there is no respite. Up and down. Up and down. I am exhausted. All I can say is it is worse than childbirth – wetter, more painful and much, much more humiliating and you are only expected to do that once or twice.

The man says I have to do ten widths twice a day and then he will come back and do the next stage. I am modestly hopeful that one day I shall be able to swim on top of the water. Only being able to swim beneath the surface is limiting my distance swimming. The Man says that if I prefer I can swim lengths. I do not prefer.

After this I sit on the terrace while David and The Man chat over more drinks as though nothing has happened. They do not realise the full import of the events of the last hour. As a child I was the dark, thin one who couldn't swim. My sister was the blond, fat one who was a good swimmer. I am putting on weight, the sun is bleaching my hair and now I can swim, under water. Apart from the sickness that threatens to engulf me having taken in so much salt water I am rightly shocked at having turned on its head our entire family writ-in-stone history. Like a Fay Weldon heroine, I am turning into my sister.

As I sit in the car looking out on to the English Channel, or where I guess it might be, I wonder if I should attempt to be the first person to swim it under the surface. Or shall I wait for The Girl to return, smuggle her through passport control and take the easier route through the tunnel?

We arrive in France in the early hours of the morning and I have to wear a blanket over my head at the hotel to arrive and leave because I might be recognised by another guest. This is madness. Our drive down through France which should take little more than an hour is six hours because The Girl has never driven on the right-hand side of the road; we have to go on minor roads 'because of the tabloids' who its seems stalk motorways here too, and although she is exhausted she cannot get help from me who knows France so well because I must not know where we are going.

Later that day after more mishaps than a Hugh Grant movie, we are at our destination which is in lovely Monet country and are picking dead or deadish creatures out of our beds in a dreadful rented cottage. I am expected to stay here for two weeks. I can feel the mould creeping towards me. It would be cruelty to unpack my pink tissue paper wrapped parcels of new clothes. The Girl is pretty dismayed too. I sleep on the bed fully clothed.

The morning sees me in a decisive mood. I have my cases at the door. I have written a note – at this stage I still have pen and paper – which I have posted under the door of our neighbours, an English family, who look like their lives could do with a bit of an adventure. The note asks for a lift into town to the decent hotel we passed on the way. I can get home from there. I lay out breakfast and wait three hours for The Girl to get up. This is my first, but not last, experience that the young are vampires – they really do not like daylight. Or is she Big Brother personified and not responding to my gentle calls on principle?

I issue an ultimatum. 'We can go back together or I will make my way back alone. You choose but I go in an hour.' I pass the time by laying out breakfast for her. I put flowers in a mug and fold a tissue into a napkin. Disconcertingly, the girl takes a photograph of the table. I keep our conversation simple, calm, even friendly. No reason for it not to be. She telephones H.Q. They telephone her. Backwards and forwards. I hate cheap mobile phones in France in an absolute deluge. We agree that she should drop me off at Paddington. It all takes forever and is tedious but I know that so much of Big Brother is tiresome and I am on the home straight. Home.

In the next two weeks I learn a valuable lesson. It is impossible to give away money to the British public.

The trains returning me to Tetbury are a mess. I have a huge and heavy suitcase and toiletries for three months as well as hand luggage and I haven't eaten or had a proper drink for days. Now I have to change trains and get across a bridge and one minute to do it. The train is full of rugby fans making their way home from Twickenham. I say to two of them, big lads holding plastic pint pots of lager, 'Get me and my luggage off this train and on to that and I will give you this twenty pound note.' Without a word they pick up me and my bags and carry us all along platforms and over the bridge. As the train guard sees us he firmly shuts the doors in our faces. A swift word or two and a gesture from The Lads and he, wisely in my opinion, opens them again. The Lads fling me and my luggage through the open door. As I fly through the air they vehemently refuse the money, 'It would be a bad show if we couldn't help a lady.' Most impressively not a drop of lager was spilt throughout this.

Worryingly, though, as I fall into the carriage I put out my arms to cushion my fall and they land on the ample chest of a seated girl. Each hand rests on each breast. I am apologetic and say, 'On top of everything else...Big Brother...running away...the disgrace...letting everyone down...I have now indecently assaulted a girl on a train.' We are all laughing and the lads show me photographs of their children and I am relieved to be back in the land of the normal. It is the best laugh I have had in months. Thank you, lovely girl and lads of Gloucester.

That is Big Brother blown out of the water, then.

Back in Tetbury I fester. I have spent nearly five months of my life getting ready for this project and now it's all over without ever happening. I shall have to turn to Plan B.

I spend the next two days mooching around. I've unpacked and although everyone is glad I'm back, it's obvious that our lengthy plans were going to mean things were going to run well in my absence. I am just not as relieved as I should be. Superfluous. With a huge sense of unfinished business. And a load of cheap toiletries and black and white clothes.

I talk to Big Brother. I walk the streets of Tetbury. I talk to Big Brother.

The next time, a week later, They came for me. Another girl, another drive, another country. North Wales this time. I am keen. I want to do this thing. Big Brother has given me a sign that they know I can be bought as this time we are in a lovely country house hotel. I am super co-operative. The Girl has various tasks for me. I paint mugs, t-shirts, views from the bedroom window, paintings of myself, I am filmed singing a song, I take photographs...we rush through her list. I wonder what the hotel staff must think as they clean our room and see the playgroup activities and equipment that are the tools of Big Brother.

I am relishing the challenge of breaking the rules. At the motorway service station on the way to Wales I claim I need the loo and refuse this time to be locked in the car. In the cubicle I write a note on loo paper and put it in a pre-addressed and stamped envelope which I have previously secreted in my magic knickers. While The Girl goes into the loo I silently slip out and accost a man in some sort of uniform. A bus driver. I ask about post boxes. There are none. I wave a ten-pound note at him and ask if he will post this letter for me. There is much tugging and pulling backwards and forwards as he refuses to take either the money or the envelope. I insist, he desists and I am looking over my shoulder for The Girl. Finally he takes the letter and I keep the ten pounds. David gets the letter.

At the hotel I test the room telephone. It has been disconnected. I wonder how Big Brother has managed this but know them to be all-powerful. The Girl, who I like, takes a bath and I slip out of the room, wedging the door open as I go as I have no key to get back, and I run down to reception. The hotel owner is there. I ask to use the phone. He says to use the one in the room. I say it is not working. He says it will be repaired. I say let me use yours. He says, reluctantly, 'O.K.' I say that I will pay now. He says no. I say yes. He says he will put it on the bill. I say no. I say I will pay now. Here is a ten-pound note. The one I don't seem to be able to get rid of. No, he says. I say put it in the charity box. In the owner's office I telephone David. We talk hurriedly. We are both all right. That's all we need to know. It is all terribly exciting. I have spoken with David and I am happy. This spying thing suits me. I run up to the room and hope that The Girl doesn't notice that I am breathless and happy.

The Big Phone call comes. The Grande Fromage telephones. I have been Chosen. I am filmed several times taking the now imaginary call. I am expected to be very excited. I leave extrovert behaviour of that sort to others who can also do bikinis and nude photo-shoots.

This is an extraordinary situation, as I have no one with whom to share this news.

In the bathroom I write a note to David telling him what is happening. We pack up. We are going to London. The Girl checks the room, sweeping it like MI5, but I double-back and put my letter under my pillow with a note saying, 'please post' but without the ten pound note as no-one is interested in it. My letter arrives in Tetbury the next morning. So much for Them trying to wean me off David.

How does the Chosen One feel? Relieved. There is no turning back now. Bring it on. I just want to get there and get on with it. In spite of all the thinking and preparation, or because of it, I think I was more ready for this back in January than now. I haven't been allowed to see newspapers or television but I know from my time 'on the run' that tomorrow is the First Night. The Girl, always efficient, is getting tense. She drives in to London and I am taken to the back of a hotel near Regents Park. I am swiftly moved through the corridors surrounded by people to shield me from any onlooker. I don't feel special, just hunted. Another basic hotel room. Curtains kept tightly closed. It's going to be a long day.

It is as well The Girl and I ate well in Wales. No stinting on some good wine either.

Everything seems to take forever. The bag inspection is hours. More Girls. All my possessions are spread out on the bed. They have brought two cases – a huge black plastic one and a smaller horrid grey shoulder bag. What I am allowed to take into the House will go in to the black case. One set of day clothes, one set of nightclothes and makeup and toiletries are to go into the grey case which is to stay with me. It will be a squeeze. The rest, 'holiday' clothes and confiscated stuff will go into my own case which will be sealed and taken away until September, or whenever.

I am intrigued by all this. This is what I came for – to see the nitty gritty dynamics, to find out for myself how it works. I am also motivated by a desire to find out how I react in such an alien situation. Unexpected things upset me. I don't mind when things are confiscated. I have taken the precaution of including some items that I know are not going to be allowed – a book, 'Nineteen Eighty Four', of course, my diary (expurgated edition with friends' addresses removed) and more t-shirts than anyone could need. Sadly my pink tissue paper is confiscated, as is an eye pencil. They think I might write the great British novel. I wish.

When I see later what the other contestants take in I can see how easy I have made it for the team.

There must be no branding, well not to the untrained eye. All toiletries are banned, except one each of basics so all that dragging them around for weeks has been a waste. I don't know what happens when these run out. Those that I can keep are wrapped in gaffer tape so no one knows what brands I use. The girls doing the garment checking are rigorous. Every inch of every item is handled. It wouldn't be easy to get drugs or such-like into the House. The Girls pack my suitcase. The Girl who came to Wales is always with me. She manages by ruthless selection to cram the smaller case with enough to see me through until the bigger case is delivered to the House, whenever that might be. It seems I am to carry this in to the House with me. I can barely lift it. We cut off the shoulder strap. The Girl says that under no circumstances am I to put it on the ground when I make my entry. By now my watch has been taken away, there are no clocks and I could, without my inbuilt time clock, have completely lost all sense of time and place.

I have borne this part of the process better than I would have thought. I like small victories although I suspect these are programmed in. There is a tussle over a packet of antiseptic surface wipes but they finally give in which is just as well as they turn out to be a life saver. They look at my knickers, just two pairs of black, two pairs of white, two black bras, two white bras – sports bras, nothing sexy. I intend to hand wash my things at night. It won't be difficult to dry things through the summer. Overall I am delighted with what I have brought in and, in fairness, I have to say The Girls are quite sensitive. However, the handling of my clothes and makeup and jewellery is strangely disturbing. Perhaps younger women or those who have lived communally, or still at home, wouldn't find this so difficult. I don't like it when they examine my jewellery, jewellery that David bought me, inspecting it closely, describing it in detail for the list they make. I, too, have made lists of everything I have brought. As should be expected of me.

I have been given no guidance on what to wear on the Launch Night. Daft of me to imagine I would be, since I have never in the last few months been told anything from one moment to the next. There is never any feedback about anything. The Big Brother Brick Wall. I am to be taken from the room for a photo shoot and, in the absence now of any other clothes, I wear the launch outfit. Just as well because these are the major promotional photographs that I am going to be stuck with all my life. It's almost as though they want to catch you out.

This is the bit I love. However tired and frustrated I am, I try to turn it on for the camera. I am not talking about the outcome which is always cringe worthy. I'm talking about the process, me watching them and that split second when the producers and cameramen ask you to do it and you do. When you give them what they want or try to. A deep-seated desire to please, perhaps, but intoxicating. I respect the makeup girls, the camera crews, the photographers and the back-up boys and girls who make tea and run errands. The least I can do is make them laugh and joke and be pleasant and try to make their lives easier. How strange it must be on this assignment to see such a disparate group of people parade in front of them.

It's late now. The Girl and I are alone in the room. People have been asking me all day if I am excited. I feel that I am the least excited person in this whole exercise. But I am absorbed by it, fascinated by the whole process. I came for this.

My co-operation is pushed to its limits when late that night when we are thinking of bed a doctor is brought to the room. They have all my medical records from my G.P. This is for the Production Company's health insurance, not for my benefit. I feel used. My mother used to say that a gentleman is someone who is never unintentionally rude. That must make me some gentleman. Whether it is the lateness of the hour, stress, or the insulting nature of her questions – she is fat and unhealthy-looking herself – I could shove her stethoscope...

Finally The Girl and I are alone. We eat a bit and watch a film, 'Lost in Translation'. A story of alienation and despair. Appropriate. Perhaps we sleep. Perhaps not.

CHAPTER FIVE

May 30th 2007. Big Brother 8. It is Launch Day.

We leave the London hotel early in the morning. I am smuggled to a car and learn that The Girl is driving me. I hope that she will stay with me until the last moment. I know that she is One Of Them, working for the Inner Party, but she has a knack of being quiet – the good sense to know when not to speak – and I like her. It is not Stockholm syndrome but it is a comfort.

In the car I have to put on a plain white mask that completely covers my face and a towel over my head. We are driving, I guess, through North London. At one stage the car stops and I peep out. We are at a zebra crossing. A mother and small child are crossing the road. The child sees me and on his face is a look of sheer horror. I want to tear off the mask and reassure him. His mother, unseeing, hurries him across the road. She will never know that all his adult neuroses started at that moment. I think of Charles Dickens. What would he have made of all this? He would have loved the magic of television and the sheer circus of this programme. He did have an absolute fear and terror of, and therefore fascination, with masks. The mask would certainly be his Room 101.

The Girl tells me we are 'there' and I assume it is the studio. Many hands lead me, blind, into a building and into a room. I can remove the towel and the mask. The room is tiny and in what I guess is a single storey Crittal windowed block. It has been a first aid room and at least has a rough bed and a shabby loo in the corner. The Girl stays with me.

It is a day for more filming. People bring lights and cameras and crowd into the small space. They ask me questions, the

70

same old questions – if you were a fruit what would it be? – and then a different set of people take their place and there is more filming and the same old questions. I'm getting increasingly scruffy and just hope I can pull everything together for opening night. I have never seen it, this long-awaited show starter, and have no idea what to expect.

Throughout the day my saliva is tested. I can't eat or drink or clean my teeth because every so often I have to chew on a piece of cotton wool which the Girl then puts in to a plastic bag and I have to fill in a form which is supposed to test my mood at the moment of cotton wool chewing.

My mood would improve if people would stop coming in to my cell and asking if I am excited.

The situation is extraordinary. I do not feel that I am about to be a celebrity, famous and feted. This doesn't feel that I am about to embark on something good or fun. I feel as though I have done something incredibly wicked, a dreadful crime, and that everyone is deeply ashamed of me. Worst of all I can't think what the crime is and, like all incarcerated prisoners, I cry inside myself that I am innocent. The cell-like room, barely clean, reinforces that.

Then a little glimmer of humour. I had decided that the hygiene in the House might not be up to scratch so I have put aside my contact lenses. I guess, too, that this better suits Big Brother's concept of me and the image I have chosen to project. As though I have a choice. My spectacles were broken last week and new ones have been ordered. My eyesight is so poor – it always has been – that I cannot get off-the-shelf glasses and they have to be made especially for me. There is a controlled panic as it would be preferable, given the complexity of the stairs that I should at least be able to see.

One of the production team comes to see me with good news. She has telephoned David and he has collected the new spectacles from the optician in Tetbury. She has sent a courier down to collect them. She tells me the conversation. She asks David what time the courier should call at the house. David says, 'Not at 11 because I'm having my hair cut.' Although I have insisted that contact with my family be kept to an absolute minimum the team knows that this may not be a typical contestant family. While the team and the world may think that Launch Night is the most important event in the history of the universe, for David it is insignificant in the face of his more critical haircut. 'When then?' 'Well after that I shall be having lunch. Let's say after 2.00 but before 3.00.' She asks if he would like to come to Elstree that evening. Special arrangements are made for relatives. 'What you have to understand,' he says, 'is that I am a very busy man.' Relenting somewhat he adds, 'But I may watch it on television.' I glow with pride. That's my man!

David follows instructions and removes all packaging and identification and they arrive safely in the box. They are a colour and style that is new to me. But, hey, who's looking?

The lining of the box has been cut with a razor and hidden inside is one of David's cards with words of love. We are not afraid of sentiment but stop short, I hope, of sentimentality. I tear the card in to small pieces. I don't want to take any piece of home in to the house. This is something I have to do alone.

The note reminds me at that moment of the early days of our relationship. David was to be on a building site all day and I put together a packed lunch in a plastic box. Hard to imagine but we do crazy things in those mad beginnings. Me and plastic boxes and packed lunches! I put in an explicit note with a small drawing. When he came back that evening we found that he had left the box on site. Remembering the graphic love note he telephoned the builders, all the contractors, the civil engineers, the other architects. I have never since heard him so officious and bombastic, something he never is with colleagues. 'Find the box and do not, do not, open it.' Or it would be fifty years of a distinguished reputation down the pan in that one little stick drawing. Still you don't marry a woman 22 years younger than yourself so as to have a quiet life – a thought that keeps me going in my cell.

It must be late afternoon and in to the room come the three Biggest Cheeses of the production team. The very nearly a heartthrob sits on the manky bed with me. Be still my beating heart. He reads loudly and slowly from a sheet. It is the Rules Inside the Big Brother House. There are twelve fundamental rules. I shall always remember them.

There is no contact with the outside world.

You are filmed 24 hours a day and must wear the personal microphone at all times.

The Diary room is the only place where you can speak with Big Brother and visits to the diary room are compulsory.

Proper reasons must be given for nominations and nominations must not be discussed.

The public decides who is evicted.

You mustn't threaten or use physical violence towards anyone else in the house.

Big Brother will throw you out if you break the rules, threaten or use physical violence, unacceptable way of behaviour that can cause offence to fellow housemates and/or to the viewing public.

Tasks are compulsory.

You mustn't move furniture or do tampering.

You must get up when you hear the alarm.

You mustn't discuss any previous series of Big Brother or Celebrity Big Brother or any of the Production Team.

Big Brother can change the rules at any time.

It all seems straightforward to me though the rebel in me now feels I want to do a bit of furniture re-arranging and general tampering.

He then elaborates on what constitutes unacceptable behaviour. I am really enjoying this because, at heart, I am rather keen on these sorts of frameworks and I can see that they will work to my benefit. I think of Winston. He says that the best books are the ones that tell you what you already know.

Unacceptable behaviour includes violent behaviour to another housemate including threats and actual violence

Behaving in a way that could cause offence to either their fellow housemates or members of the viewing public – this on includes offence on grounds of age, sex, disability, gender, race, religion, beliefs or sexual orientation

Serious harassment and bullying

Intentionally plugging brand names

Saying anything that is calculated to bring Big Brother and the producers into disrepute

Damaging the house or contents

Making false or libellous allegations

A major infringement of the Big Brother rules

Misleading Big Brother before coming into the house.

Anything else Big Brother considers serious enough.

Fair enough, squire. Only a fool wouldn't listen and take it on board. It's not just what Big Brother thinks, or other housemates, it's what the whole world thinks that matters. I'm no fool. I will have people looking in at me whose good opinion is vital to me. I cannot afford to let them down. Or myself.

I sign this document and the contract between the production company and me.

I would like them, the producers, to give me some sign of approval or encouragement. I don't need it but it would just help. There's nothing there. No warmth. But they did get me my spectacles and that counts for a lot.

I decide to get changed into my outfit. We, The Girl and I, have been sent a last supper. Something heavy in polystyrene containers. Neither of us can eat. She goes away to pace the walk and someone takes her place to guard me. The Girl is my understudy in a sense and she goes to rehearse what I have to do. I wash and change in the cramped and inadequate space. There is a tiny mirror stuck high on the wall. I am the least vain woman in the world, with good reason, but I wish the facilities were better. They do keep telling me I should be excited so the surroundings might just have made it easier. I do what I can with my makeup. I am dressed – thank you, Caroline Charles – and ready. I should imagine it's a bit like going to a

White House dinner from a tent on a campsite, though I have been to neither.

The Girl returns and tells me about the walk from the car. I am to carry the case which I must not put down. I don't ask for explanations I am too busy memorising what she tells me. I just assume it will explode. The pathway is narrow with barriers on each side. There are steps, she counts them for me but I can't hear and I instantly forget. I must stop at the top and turn and pose. We practice the walk. She is very good at it. I have to carry the ten ton bag, walk putting one foot directly in front of the other to minimize my size; I must look back over my shoulder, lower my spectacles with one hand, and raise my eyebrows.

I shall never remember all this. I can envisage myself wondering off down the wrong road like an old person escaped from a nursing home.

There is a C.D. player in the cell pumping out garage or indie or something. It must never be turned off because I must not be heard in another cell. I have a slight headache from this. The Girl changes into a simple black trouser suit. She looks wonderful. Perhaps she can take my place.

There is shouting. 'We're ready! We're ready.' Over and over again. We stand by the door. Two security guards sweep in and search me. Hands everywhere. I have no time to dwell as there is a final saliva test and last questionnaire. The Girl looks nervous. She can't afford for anything to go wrong now. I focus on her. I won't let you down.

Waiting and waiting. I can hear screaming in the near distance. Someone comes and puts a microphone on me. I am warned about the cost of this equipment and I mustn't damage it. Someone else comes in and puts earplugs in my ears. Someone else puts earphones over my ears. Someone else puts a mask over my spectacles. Deaf and blind I am led, half-carried from the room. The Girl holds my hand. I squeeze it to reassure her. I am put in to a car. Music is playing so loudly that I can hear it and the vehicle throbs. I am in the back of the car and a man keeps shouting at me, 'Don't peep. Don't peep.' I think what an odd little word. Peep. I'm not peeping. I'm trying to breathe.

After an age the car is moving, swiftly but just a few yards I guess. The earmuffs and eye mask are dragged from me. I pull out the earplugs and The Girl, her voice uncharacteristically rough and loud, and others, shout, 'Get out. Get out.'

I grab the exploding case and step from the car.

CHAPTER SIX

Joan Bakewell says that when women get to a certain age they become invisible, though it doesn't seem to me that Joan herself is particularly invisible. She is also reported as saying that she regrets not having slept with more people when she was young. The only point on which we differ is that I think it's not too late to change these things.

I have been bound and gagged, literally, and for the last few hours have been confined in a small space deprived of all the rights that make us free individuals. I have undergone procedures and processes that have been humiliating and intrusive. After a lifetime of working hard to make myself, and those around me, comfortable I have endured more discomfort in the last few months than in the previous 60 years, at a time when I don't need to. For months, too, I have had the burden of unaccustomed secrecy haunting me day and night with its constant underlying responsibility for what my actions might bring down on others. Unspecified fears, largely. Plus an uncertainty about my future, a completely uncharacteristic dithering for the first time in my life. For months I have been, as they say, 'out of my comfort zone'.

I step from the car.

It might appear to the onlooker as though I were walking into madness. They might think that I had been cosseted, diva-like, in luxury, pandered to, adored in advance, groomed for this moment just to step confidently into the maelstrom. It isn't like that. I felt as though I were stepping **from** an insane world into sanity. The sense of release is enormous and I can quite see how younger, more excitable people go mad, according to the

Big Brother script, and give the audience the extrovert red carpet show that Launch Night is all about.

I stand by the car for a second. I am surprised by how close everyone is to me. I am surrounded by what seems like hundreds of men with cameras. Lights are flashing everywhere. I smile and wave to them. Simple really. These must be the newspapermen and paparazzi. The people we have spent months evading, travelling on B roads, hiding under blankets, and for whom we have lied to friends and family and strangers. Now we are face to face. Or would be if it weren't for the flashing lights. I don't know what all the fuss was about. They are totally charming. They call my name. Not Lesley Brain or Mrs Brain as one would expect from strangers, but Lesley. 'Lesley' coming at me from all sides. Very pleasantly shouted. Extremely friendly. Do I know you? I want to reach out my hand and shake theirs as would be polite under any other social circumstances. Except they are not content with one photograph when a hundred will do. I like them and can't imagine why they are considered such big bad wolves.

I move along the narrow corridor between the two barriers. People reach out to touch me and they are all smiling and happy and calling to me in a jocular way.

I feel incredibly small, physically tiny. And contained. I have neatly defined edges, all crisp and brisk.

I can hear a voice talking about me and I recognise it as Davina, the presenter of the series. Her voice booms out, echoing around me from somewhere on high. Davina is considered a saint and star by most Big Brother aficionados and one of the holy grails of the whole adventure. I don't know if I am walking towards a meeting with Davina. I rather hope so as I would like to meet her and have a chat. She sounds authoritative, as though she knows a lot about me and I would like to reciprocate and get to know her. I don't suppose it works like that. I hear her say, 'Charles and Camilla and Charles Dickens' and wonder if they are coming too.

At one time it was considered a sign of madness to believe that the earth goes round the sun. Today it is madness to believe that the past is unalterable. God can't change the past but Big Brother can. Thank you, Big Brother. I like the sound of my new past.

I look up and there is a big screen with me on it playing golf outside our utility room. Ridiculous. I haven't time to stop as I have the steps to negotiate and there's no handrail. I am glad I'm wearing pumps. I am standing on a round glass dais lit from below. I am happy I chose trousers. In fact I feel very comfortable about it all. I remember to stand still for a moment and do a little look over my shoulder for The Girl and, miraculously, I raise my eyebrows. I feel relaxed and happy. My thinking is calm and entirely under my control. It vaguely surprises me that all these people and those in the wider audience should be interested, but I know they haven't come to see me but the other, more showy, contestants. In the split second that I do a twirlette on the podium, as I wave to the cheering and friendly crowd, an uncontrolled, unbidden thought comes into my mind. It is louder and more insistent than my immediate preoccupation with not letting down the producers by falling over – though I haven't ruled out that they have put it in to my head, a person who to date has never fallen over, because that is what they want to happen.

I WILL NEVER BE MORE FAMOUS THAN I AM AT THIS MOMENT.

I turn and there are steeper stairs to negotiate but with a handrail. Recklessly, perhaps too relaxed, I shift the heavy bag from one hand to another. I am on a scaffold walkway. It all looks a bit makeshift to me but, being married to an architect, I am quite at home on building sites. I am standing at the first entrance door to the Big Brother House. The Girl said the door will open automatically and after that I am on my own. Instinctively I turn and wave to the crowd. Not a big extravagant gesture just a wave, elbow tightly to the side of my body, and I blow a kiss. Where it fell I cannot tell. I turn and walk through the open doors which swiftly close behind me.

I never once believed that all those people have come to see me or that those cameras are because of me. That would be the certain route to real madness. I see myself as having a small supporting non-speaking role in a huge production. One in the crowd scene in Ben Hur perhaps. My job is to follow the very few instructions I have been given, to listen carefully to my own instincts about timing, and generally not make an arse of myself.

The audience watching there, or on television, or tape later can judge my performance and me for themselves. What they can't do is to know what those few minutes feel like. Only by doing it can you know. That is why I am there.

IT'S FANTASTIC. I use that word carefully. I get infuriated when that word is used to describe holidays in Cornwall or trips to the shopping centre. It is a word we never use in our family. Far too exaggerated, too over the top. It doesn't, however, come even close to describing the experience of that walk. Talk to the hundred and twenty or so people who have done the Big Brother entrance walk and I am sure the story would be the same. Although by design contestants are totally different they will have the shared experience of that moment. Whatever they have done before or since, whatever our ambitions and fantasies it will always be the most fantastic experience of our lives. In the days that follow we, the contestants, re-enact the moments to each other to re-run and try to capture just a glimpse of that feeling.

When the doors close behind me it is suddenly quiet. The roar of the crowd is already just a memory. My moment of fame is gone, probably forever. I am in a brightly lit corridor with steep stairs. I breathe deeply and descend. There is a door that I have been told I must open myself. I wonder where the team got the idea that I have a problem with stairs and doors. Perhaps their concern is not confined to me. I mustn't take it personally. I did hear talk of someone in a previous show falling. I am in an inner lobby, vestibule my mother would call it, completely covered floor and ceiling in black and white tiles. The room and my clothes are co-ordinated. A little accent of red would have been good. There are mirrors in the room which I guess conceal the cameras. I push another door which opens into the sitting room of The House.

Except, of course, it isn't a house. It's a television set, a gaudy, transient bauble. Then right in my face bobbing up and down, screaming in high pitched sounds are two pink fluffy giraffes licking round lollies on sticks, little Lolitas, up and down, like Masai warriors but speaking some totally unintelligible 'language'. 'Girlies,' I say. I make out that they are saying they are twins to which I say 'uncanny,' but really I think they are probably good friends who, like children do, choose to dress alike. They appear to me to be facially very different. They are absolutely charming to me and I take it they are hostesses. I am hopeful because behind them on a kitchen island I can spot glasses and two bottles. The hostesses – it never occurs to me that they might be contestants – show no sign of offering me a drink, and I could do with a really stiff one, and they start indicating features of the room.

I have been in the house (I have dropped the capital letter as this cardboard and plastic monstrosity doesn't warrant it) for thirty seconds and, looking past the ever-bobbing creatures, I can see A Big Problem.

The bedroom is a dormitory, as I had expected, but there are huge multi-occupancy beds. In the far corner I can spy a little single bed. Mine. I shall need to have my wits about me.

I tell the girls they are beautiful and they are. So new and unblemished, like giant children. They tower above me on great high-heeled shoes borrowed from the dressing up box. They show me the bath in the sitting room and the cooker in the bedroom. No wonder we haven't had many laughs en route, Big Brother and I. We don't laugh at the same things. I want that drink but the hostesses seem a bit lax in that department so I help myself, and them. I have cracked their language.

Pink. Pink. See I can speak it too. I am not seriously worried when I realize at last that they are housemates. While I have little to say on the subject of pink – they will never have heard of Pink Floyd – they are not girls to take that amiss being so sweet and gentle and forgiving by nature. They will win this show, I decide. Deffo.

By contrast the next contestant looks more challenging. Another giant on stilettos with legs longer than I am, wearing tiny shorts and a man's shirt. I am uncertain if it is a man or woman, or a bit of both and the name Charley doesn't help much. 'A boy's name,' I say, hoping for clarification. Receiving none I open the 'champagne' instead. Charley is much concerned about having been booed by the crowd outside. It had never occurred to me that I might be booed by strangers. Charley is what is called in modern parlance, 'hot', which I think means sexy and aggressive.

Tracey is next. She will be popular with the 'twins' as she has pink hair. Dressed for Glastonbury in the 80's she, too, talks a strange language. The house is 'fat' and 'gravy'. The first impression is that she is highly energetic. I wonder if that will wear off. I wonder, too, if all this might all be a bit too main-stream for an old raver.

They are coming thick and fast now. A pretty girl from Yorkshire with a slight resemblance to Victoria Beckham. She has a frightened look in her eyes that looks like it might have been there a long time. She is appalled by her own swearing and so repeats the obscenity over and over again.

I can't remember their names now and I can see the 'champagne' is going to run out. I quickly refill my glass just in case.

A Welsh girl with lovely thick dark hair and beautiful eyes...a conventionally pretty blond wearing a sad little Orphan Annie dress and sporting a loud, confident voice...a lovely Indian girl who looks terrified but I think that will pass...

'Where are the men?' Am I the only one to notice there are no men?

I am reluctant to press the point, still retaining a tiny glimmer of hope, and no one would hear me anyway. They all shout. Especially an Amy Winehouse look-alike who shouts loudest of all and, taking us all in in one look, declares she will form us in to a girl-band. I think I will present even this dynamic and forceful girl with too great a challenge. There is an older lady, my age or more, an East Londoner who looks a tad over-excited for her age and should therefore fit in well enough. Because, standing back and watching, I can see that as they shout and scream and pay each other compliments they are eyeing each other up and assessing and judging. And the prize will go to that girl judged best looking and by their definition only the young are eligible. It is like animals of the same species meeting in the jungle. Some of us would never have been in the competition. When I spoke to Charley – I have decided she is a girl – she looked straight past me into one of the mirrors as we spoke. As far as my relationship with Charley is concerned I would be well advised to take up bank robbing with her as the only witness. She would never be able to identify me.

As the housemates come my heart sinks. I never realistically expected Andrew Marr or Peter Ackroyd but really Big Brother, did you have to do this to me? I am up for a challenge, but this? You have put me straight in to my own personal Room 101. I salute you for your cruelty.

I move over to Big Brother's idea of a joke. A Dali-esque telephone with a plastic lobster. I pick it up and speaking in to the dead thing ask for a taxi. I am not joking.

As I turn back to the ominous drinks – eleven people, two bottles doesn't auger well for the catering arrangements – I think I catch sight of a shadow at the window. A fleeting glimpse, more a memory than a reality. It's my friend, Charles Dickens. In my minds eye I see him more clearly now with paper and a quill pen. He's writing furiously. Two Barbie dolls, a snooty old lady, a transsexual who isn't, a time-travelled raver, a footballer's wife, a screaming Banshee, an Orphan

Annie, a Welsh Matt Lucas and a bearded lady. Forget Nicholas Nickleby and his travelling band of actors. Forget the freak shows and the circuses. Even you, with all your genius, couldn't have made this up, Mr.Dickens.

We stand about not knowing what to do, so the girls talk about breasts. Or, in Chanelle's case, lack of breasts. She furkles down her dress and produces two small plastic bags full of a jelly substance. These are called chicken fillets, I am told. They are passed around for all to handle. There is much exclaiming about her Victoria likeness and when she strikes her 'pose' for which she tells us she is famous in Leeds, I can see it myself. She knows everything there is to know about the Beckhams which, given my ferreting around the private lives of the Victorian writers, I can identify with; the difference is she actually wants to be Victoria and I can't quite see me modelling myself on Mrs Dickens. The talk about breasts goes on. We are all invited to test the weight of the Welsh girl's breasts with our hands. Apparently they are as heavy as they look.

There is talk of reduction operations and the conversation enters an intimacy with which I am unfamiliar at cocktail parties – or anywhere else for that matter. Laura introduces herself but tells me that people generally call her 'Wangers'. I have to ask her to repeat herself. This not being able to understand what people are saying is going to be a big problem and could get me in to trouble. They speak in regional accents – no great difficulty there – but very, very fast, extremely loudly, and they use vocabulary that is entirely new to me. They seem to have no problem understanding each other despite their differences. I am going to have to work hard to understand them although even at this early stage I can see they would never reciprocate the effort. To be marginalized by the way one looks, one's manner, one's voice and vocabulary is something that is new to me, certainly in such an obvious way. I am going to have to tread carefully. 'People call me Wangers on account of my big tits,' says Laura. She obligingly spells it out to me. 'W.A.N.G.E.R.S.' I try it out for sound. 'And do you like that?'

I never get an answer. I suppose that like a Greek philosopher my genius lies in the questions I ask.

Each new discovery causes the girls to scream. The fridge is in the garden. The cooker is in the bedroom. The pool. The pink mugs. It is all screaming. I find some strawberries and begin to prepare them for us all. Keep calm, Lesley, and have a strawberry. They smell of fish.

I am terribly aware of cameras.

They don't seem to have noticed that there are no men. They haven't been curious about the mirrors except to stare in to them constantly. 'Oh, I'm sorry, I was just looking at how beautiful I am,' says Shabs. They are indifferent to the microphones. They haven't acknowledged the cameras set everywhere, moving as we move to capture every action, every nuance of my face. If they could see inside my head, which I think Big Brother can, they would see that it is the tiny bed that preoccupies me. As soon as the loudspeaker declares that the bedroom door is open I grab my case and dash through it like Linford Christie. Not seriously challenged at that time I fling my bag on to the single bed while the others whoop and throw themselves about. I declare, 'The single bed is mine. It was agreed with the production company.' I think I got away with it for the moment. I don't really care what they think about this. It is entirely non-negotiable.

We find a bathroom. A girlie sort of place with a settee, old-fashioned hairdryers and two steam tubs. Chanelle and I stand and look with differing amazement. I think that whoever designed this place has solved that age-old problem that besets designers and architects. That of form and function. Which takes priority? This place probably has neither. Though not wishing to judge too soon, I rather like Chanelle and think we might get on. I sense that, putting aside the Victoria Beckham fantasy, we may have something in common. Admiring the bathroom she says, 'How long would this take to build?' I like the way she asks me. The others aren't going to consult me in this way. 'I would say not very long given the finish. Mine is a little more permanent than this. I think that's the best way of putting it.' The building trade is one area of life where you really do get what you deserve. I don't want to sound too negative in the face of all their enthusiasms but I suspect that Chanelle can be encouraged to wish for better in life. I sense, too, that she would stop at nothing to get what she wants.

I have already put my foot in it with Tracey. As she and I stood looking at the nasty sitting room which I had already condemned as 'hardly Lutyens', I remarked to Tracey, who I felt instinctively despite our appearances might share a kindred spirit, 'It's terribly manky.' Tracey was indignant, 'It can't be manky. It's brand new.' I realized then that I should, out of politeness, tread carefully. Life, as I am learning, is a comparative exercise.

I am feeling better now the bed matter is settled. There is a bit of mild rumbling about it but no fuss about their bed sharing. All girls together. I hear 'old woman' and that's all right. I would have insisted upon the single bed when I was 18 but they don't need to know that. It is a question of attitude, not age.

There is nothing to unpack as we won't get our suitcases today so I sit down to chat and get to know my housemates. I could, if I play my cards right, be spending thirteen weeks with them. It is tricky. I decide to start with the language. I am sitting with Tracey who I learn is a professional cleaner from Cambridgeshire which I know well. We talk about Cambridge and Newmarket and I think I know her local pub. Emboldened by this and her good nature I ask if I might ask a question. She seems genuinely pleased. 'Can you tell me what 'fat' means as in this is fat or that is fat?' She laughs and spells it out to me. P.H.A.T. It means really good. An alternative word is 'gravy'. It is not a rich language. Tracey has refined Newspeak without having read the book. She doesn't speak in sentences just a few limited words to cover all eventualities. This is intriguing. 'So, if there is a 'phat' is there a 'phin', like fat and thin?' I ask. It's a little early to get into the simplicity of it all but Tracey, with a laugh, resolves to teach me, if only I can learn.

Tracey is thrilled to be in the house. There is a lot of talk between the girls about their ages. Carole, Tracey and I are excluded from this on the grounds that we are too old to be of interest. Nicky, the girl of Indian origin, is pitied for being 28, or whatever. The others vie for status. Youth and looks are valued above everything. Tracey at 38 has neither by their judgement. She sees this Big Brother house as her big chance despite her age. Tracey will win this. Deffo.

We gather together at the dining table and Carole busies herself at the kitchen area. In the absence of more alcohol we settle for tea and Carole takes up what is to be her permanent position. Someone asks how old I am. It seems churlish but I really don't like the question and have a bit of a problem with the answer so decide to plump for how I feel. 'Seventy two,' I say with absolute certainty. Since Nicky, in her late twenties, is the object of pity I am interested to see what response this gets. No one is interested or surprised but Carole, handing me some tea, says she would not put me a day over 63 or 65. 'So you make tea, Carole, and give compliments. The perfect combination in a new best friend.'

Tracey, reverting to her theme of how lucky we are to be in the phat and gravy house, describes us as the 'Chosen Few'. I don't know anything about ravers, though she has explained it is about ' 'aving it in a field' but I can't see the link between the non-materialistic, free take-me-as-you-find- me world of the raver and the wannabe world of Big Brother. I shall be interested in finding out more about this. I am afraid to ask any more questions for fear of falling back on old interviewing techniques.

The girls are talking about fame. This, too, fascinates me. While this is a major topic it is Shabs – Amy Winehouse – who really obsesses. They talk incessantly about 'deals'. I don't know what these are. I never wonder if they might apply to me.

Tracey says again that we are the 'Chosen Few'. I express the thought that no one could possibly be watching the show. Could anyone find this interesting? They are oblivious to the thought of onlookers.

I am called into the Diary Room. It is my first visit. I love this part of the process. How it works. The hidden cameras, the locked doors, the waiting for Big Brother to let you in, the various voices of Big Brother. The Diary Room is the original of all those little black cardboard Diary Rooms carted around the country for auditions. The chair is plastic with an inflated seat and is lit from within with tubes. It is terribly uncomfortable. If I sit back my legs stick straight out like a child. I settle for sitting hunched up at the front. There is nothing to look at except a camera lens set roughly into the wall ahead. I end up focussing on nothing so that my head waves about like David Blunkett. They ask me questions in that slow deliberate way with long spaces between words just like the auditions. Questions. Answers. The silent, unspoken Truth.

Q: Lesley, how are you enjoying your first night in the Big Brother House?

A: It is interesting.

Truth: I hope I don't look as miserable as I feel.

Q: How did you enjoy Your Entrance?

A: It was amazing. No one could be prepared for anything like that.

Truth: I loved it and I want to do it again every day but I would die rather than give you any credit for that.

Q: What do you think of the other housemates?

A: They are vibrant and energetic. It is going to be a challenge.

Truth: They are airheads.

Q: Tell me more about your impression of the housemates.

A: They are physically very beautiful.

Truth: Why didn't you choose Miss Moggy-Moose? She was much better looking than this lot. They are manky.

Q: How is it going to be a challenge?

A: Mixing with people who are so very different from oneself is always going to be a challenge. At the moment I am culturally lost. We have no common language or cultural references.

Truth: I am going to kill someone.

Q: How are you getting on with the other housemates?

A: At present I am the person least able to integrate because of the differences, for example music.

Truth: I can't talk about deals, tits and pink.

Q: How does that make you feel?

A: Initially isolated but nothing more than that.

Truth: It's your bloody fault. O.K. I accept Andrew Marr might not have been available but you could have found someone for me to talk to.

Bastards!

Big Brother: Thank you, Lesley.

Lesley: Thank you.

I absolutely refuse to call the media studies graduates who sit behind the black cardboard screen 'Big Brother'.

Poor Winston said that, as far as he could remember, he had never in real life heard church bells ring. I suspect that most of the housemates have never heard church bells either. Metaphorically speaking, that is.

It is early morning. I am the first in bed. Bliss, the mattress is one of those memory things. I love it. The others stay up to talk more about pink and deals.

End of a perfect day.

Chapter Seven

The bedroom is pitch dark at night, indeed because it is an enclosed space with no natural light it could be dark all day and night. There is an internal light switch but there is an over-ride by Big Brother who controls everything here. The girls finally came to bed but, like over-excited children on a sleepover, which is what they are, they screamed and jumped about the bedroom until falling asleep. I would set their average age at 12, if you leave out Carole. It is silent in the dormitory except for the whirl of the air conditioning. The rooms are either stifling hot or freezing at Big Brother's whim.

After a few hours rest, I am up and ready for the day. I really am very excited about it all and want to get on with it. I feel my way in the dark to the lavatory, which is brightly lit. I am aware of the cameras following me and know that I can be seen even when I cannot see. It is an odd feeling. It feels less odd to be wearing a microphone. Using the loo is going to require judicious draping of garments. I don't wish to embarrass the young people manning the cameras. Mission accomplished, I feel my way back to the bedroom to my bed.

Except I can't find it. I feel around but it isn't there. Just a void. I stand in the middle of the room. This is what I had feared but had half expected. It was too good to be true. Big Brother has taken away the single bed. I move around and reach out a hand. I have touched someone in bed and she screams. It is Laura, the Welsh girl. Nicky wakes, too, and screams out. The rest don't stir. I turn and stumble and hit my knee. The bed, my bed, is still there. I sit on it gratefully for a while until the girls have settled again and then thread my way through shoes and clothes on the floor to the sitting room. There is a metal shutter on the window but it is raised and I try the door which is unlocked. This will be my first real look at the yard to the house, which they call a 'garden'.

My embarrassment at waking the girls is tempered by my internal time clock which never lets me down. In the outside world I always wear a watch but rarely consult it. In any case, girls, it is daylight and by the look of it we are well into the day.

Patterns of behaviour are to be established early, I find. Habits of a lifetime whether you are 18 or 80 go with you everywhere. I will get up around eight and be ready for bed at midnight. The girls will stay in bed until early afternoon. I am a sociable person who also loves time alone. I just hope the camera understands this.

The temporary loss of bed and getting up in the morning is reported to Big Brother by the girls as 'sleepwalking'. They claim to be concerned for me but they forget Big Brother saw it better than they did and it smacks of sneaking to me. Later Big Brother asks me if I sleep walk. No. In the world of these girls, getting up at 8 is called 'sleepwalking'. As Tracey would say, 'Get over it.'

The garden is a small, enclosed space with high walls made of hardboard, wooden cladding, bits of trellis and what looks like any old leftovers from a building site. There is astro-turf on the ground, a few pieces of 'contemporary' garden furniture that turn out to be as uncomfortable as they are ugly, and a tiny pool. The walls are covered with mirrors. That will please the ever-preening girls. There is a mangle. I guess that Carole will like the mangle. It is all surprisingly small. The garden and the house are neither as large nor as sleek as they appear on television. I am sure it all cost a great deal of money particularly given the cost of the technical equipment alone but the overall impression is cheap and tacky. There is nothing glamorous about it and so sense about it that we are valued.

I walk round the garden and then the sitting room, tapping on walls. This is something I learnt from David. I don't learn much from this because it is all hollow and cardboardy. It is obvious that behind each wall is a walkway for access to the cameras and for viewing us, like London zoo, as well as for maintenance. It looks as though it is possible to remove certain panels in the walls, perhaps to extend the space or bring in large items. We shall see.

There is something suspicious about the pool construction. Remember, I know something about pools. It is as though I were looking at half a pool. I tap the surrounding walls but they are as hollow as the rest. Whatever is hidden you can be sure of one thing. On the basis of what is already there I am certain it will be no more stylish or satisfactory to the eye. It is, after all, a television studio. It is not Blenheim Palace.

There are plants in the garden. Succulents mostly. I remember hearing that this house is to be destroyed at the end of the show and hope that these temporary warm weather plants will be saved. By the bench marked 'for the use of smokers' there is one little tree. A sapling. A puny thing. I touch its sad little trunk and feel its pain. I name her Gertrude, the great gardener and Lutyens' colleague. I have made my first friend.

In the fridge in the garden and in the kitchen I explore the provisions that Big Brother has left for us. These are to keep us going until we receive shopping in return for successful challenges. They reflect the tastes and good sense of the Big Brother support teams and fall pretty much in line with what I would have chosen. They will not, I predict, suit the other contestants. The kitchen is not well equipped, even to my untrained eye, but I hope there will be better things to do than naff over food. Fruit, fresh vegetables, salads - that's the way forward. I haven't forgotten my cookery lessons and, although I haven't identified a suitable recipient of my recipes, I am keen.

There is a pile of paper napkins on the side untouched, except by me, from last night's drinks and canapés. There are a couple of loo rolls in a cupboard and amongst the crisps and biscuits there is a large packet of cashew nuts. I take the napkins, one loo roll, the cashew nuts and a bar of plain chocolate and head back to the bedroom. Confident now in the dark I secrete them in a drawer under my bed. I shall find a safer place later.

Back in the kitchen I make a coffee. It is, as Big Brother planned, a nuisance that the milk is in the garden fridge but I don't mind the walk. Exercise might be a problem here. I take the mug and sit by Gertrude in the garden. I do not forget for one second that I am being filmed. I do not believe that anyone could be viewing this tosh but I know I must be aware of the Thought Police.

I plan my escape route. I have heard that it has been done before and I can already see why. It would be easy for me to scale the walls. There are plenty of footholds and most likely the wall would come down with one tug. Two weeks earlier I had completed a wall climbing experience at an event in Gloucester. I am confident. We have been shown how to activate the locks on the fire doors but I favour the more glamorous Steve McQueen escape, sans motorbike. If I fall, I fall. My mind turns morbidly to thoughts of funerals.

My experience of funerals is very limited. There was a funeral just after David and I met. 'Would you come to a funeral with me?' he asked invitingly. I agreed and dressed up for it. I looked like a Mafia widow head to toe in black and a large hat with low sweeping brim. My Father used to like a good funeral. He said that English women always dress their best at funerals and their worst at weddings. We arrived promptly at the crematorium and I was a little surprised by the fellow mourners. We were both over-dressed. We were greeted warmly and were made much of. David declined to go 'back to the house' and as we left he confided in me that he had made a mistake in the date and the funeral we were meant to be at was the next day. So, having been to no funerals in my life, on meeting David I went to two in two days.

Such funerals as we had in the family were attended by the men. The women stayed at home with the caterers or were the caterers. My parents were Atheists. Real Atheists. No sitting on fences for them. Uncle Arthur was another story. Sitting by the smokers' bench I remember Uncle Arthur as clearly as if he were with me. He was my mother's uncle but only a couple of years older than her. Photographs of him show a Modigliani figure, lean, elegant, dressed like a thin Oscar Wilde. He lived with his friend, Uncle Nobby, in a way that now in Big Brother land would require a label, an explanation, but then it all seemed to us what it was – a natural and civilised way of life. I remember their house, so different from where I sit now. A small house but a jewel.

When Nobby died nearly twenty years ago there was a great feeling of loss for Uncle Arthur. They had been together for a lifetime and in all respects it had been a marriage. Even my mother, who held no great brief for gays or death – 'I never minded until it became compulsory', I not sure which she meant – was sympathetic.

Sitting in this naff place I remember Uncle Arthur's face, all white and drawn and him being uncharacteristically verbose. It seems he had been to the undertaker to discuss the funeral arrangements. They had agreed a simple ceremony without fuss or frills. At the end of the meeting the undertaker asked Uncle Arthur if he would like to see Mr Clark's body. I can see Uncle Arthur's shudder of distaste as he told us about this. The undertaker pressed. 'Please do,' he urged. 'We find it so often helps the bereaved.' To seal the matter he added desperately, 'We have made a particularly good job with Mr Clark. Trust me.' Never trust a man who says that.

The sun is getting higher and I move away from the smoker's sign, which I don't want to be filmed beside, to the shade. There is no movement from the house. Outside, in the real world over the confining walls I can hear the sounds of every day life. I had thought the house would be deep in the countryside but it is in a built up area.

Because we are essentially nice and accommodating people we say 'yes' in our family when we should say 'no'. The Big Brother experience may well be a case in point. So, to ease the undertaker's grief, Uncle Arthur miserably agrees to view the body. The undertaker withdraws and leaves him alone for a few minutes. Uncle Arthur appears a little later, clearly shaken. He tells us that he knew he must have looked ashen. The undertaker is all apologies. 'I am so sorry. I should never have suggested that you see the deceased. But people usually do find it very helpful.' Uncle Arthur, polite to a fault, tries to comfort him. 'It is not that,' he says. 'That is not Mr Clark.'

The undertaker is adamant. 'Yes. It is. What you must understand is that people change in death. Though I must say we made a particularly good job with Mr Clark.'

Shaken but firm, Arthur says, 'But Nobby was a slight man, small even, and clean-shaven. That is a large man with a full black beard...wearing naval uniform.' The undertaker, it being his turn to be surprised, excuses himself.

He returns some considerable time later looking more discreet and sombre than ever, if that were possible. 'I am afraid I have some bad news for you,' he says. 'Mr Clark was buried yesterday with full naval honours. Admirals drove down from London and rifles were fired over his coffin.' So much for understatement.

Uncle Arthur, however, is visibly cheered. 'Nobby would have loved that,' he said. 'He was always very fond of sailors.'

Two days later the naval officer was buried in a simple ceremony. My Mother broke with family tradition and went to the funeral.

Sitting in **this** garden I plan a pet cemetery-style memorial to be erected on a piece of ground near Gertrude. It would be in memory of Big Brother contestants. There would be a large shrine, perhaps a statue of Davina draped in black marble, as a memorial to all those who auditioned over the years and weren't Chosen. There could be smaller statues of Dermot, lots of little Dermots, grouped around her feet to represent those who were Chosen but failed to win. There would be no need for a tribute to the actual winners as, from what I hear from listening to the girls, their memorial is to appear in Nuts magazine.

I have been having a lovely time and then I hear sounds in the house and go in to see what the day has to offer.

Descartes, the great French philosopher, and I have a lot in common. He spent much of his life from 1596 to 1650 – just before our Gloucestershire house was built, actually – in search of peace and quiet. In order to achieve this he chose eventually to live in Holland. A desperate measure. He would not have enjoyed this day in the Big Brother house.

The girls are awake and screaming. Although very little happens here relationships themselves are speeded up. Friendships and alliances are formed and quickly fall apart. What in normal society may take months or years here can happen in moments. Feelings are strong, people are hated or loved. Indifference over anything isn't tolerated. Roles within the house are quickly established. Conflict is in the air. Jealousy is the key motif of the house. If I were on the other side of the one-way mirror I think I would be having a ball watching this. I wouldn't waste my time with it at home, unpaid. Being here, in it, is fraught.

We are going to have a house meeting. This seems to me to be a good idea. Household tasks, which I think ought to be kept to a minimum, can be allocated and we can get on with the more important issues of fun and activities, whether of our own making or imposed on us by Big Brother. This is not how others think. It soon becomes clear that no one else in the group has any experience of meetings or indeed of decision-making and negotiating within a group. Except for Nicky. Nicky is the only person in the group who has any serious knowledge of the workplace and has, she tells me, given up a job which she has held for seven years or so to come on the show. The others are generally unemployed most of the time or are students.

Carole has already indicated that she wants a monopoly of the kitchen and household duties. While I am all for other people doing what I don't want to do, I don't feel that this is fundamentally right. Carole has told me something of her political and other activities – for some reason she doesn't work now but is busy advising others how to lead their lives – and it would not be appropriate for such an interesting person to be marginalized by this domestica. There are also others who will like to cook. It does me no good, either, to reinforce the view of the young that old people, as they are so quick to call us, are good for one thing and that is to service their needs. However, Carole's years manning the barricades, Greenham Common and membership of George Galloway's Respect party have, surprisingly, left her with a phobia about meetings. Carole is crying.

There is a lot of crying.

The high of the day before, launch day, has been followed by a deep depression. It is as though when they walked through the doors into the house the girls dropped their spirit and motivation. It is true, looking back, that I heard a little 'plop' when I came in but I think that was something else. My sense of humour, perhaps. Anyway, not having been as high as them I am not suffering the same low and think I can he helpful in the jollying along sense.

When she isn't shouting Charley, too, is crying. This is a loud, all consuming activity, which, like everything Charley does, engages all our attentions. Except Shabs, who is too much in love with herself to seriously concern herself with anyone else, but is Charley's best friend. Though I doubt that Charley would ever really have a best friend. Charley sobs and the meeting pauses. Charley is chronically incapable of wearing her microphone. Big Brother announces every five minutes that a housemate isn't wearing her microphone and we are all forced to check. Ludicrously, Charley says she wants to be a 'presenter'. I mention, kindly and helpfully, that I know nothing about it but would have thought the ability to remember to put on a microphone might be a minimum job requirement.

I know that Tracey is not going to enjoy the authority of meetings but she is, I guess, essentially a rule keeper. I suspect that like me she sees that keeping small rules leaves you more scope to break big ones. She is a professional cleaner and I think she would be brilliant at it. I have seen the neat and tidy way she lies in bed. I suggest she chairs the meeting which she does quite readily. We go round and volunteer for jobs. Carole, through her tears, wants to do everything – cooking, washing, and cleaning – so that a cynical person might think she is establishing herself as our mother earth figure. She and I have very different views on mothering. I just hope her household skills justify her self-selection. She has already told me that her own house is a tip.

I am not slow to make my offer. I will do mangling – I tell them I have practised this in the morning – I will water Gertrude and the other plants and I shall do post-modern irony, 'since someone has to'. Tracey looks at me blankly. Well, if you can have your own personal language then I can have mine.

I have sensed during this meeting, and before, that there was some issue about me beyond the obvious awkwardness of first meetings. Suddenly Carole is part of the meeting and she makes a statement. There is to be no peeing in the shower. Eyes turn to me and there is much screaming about the horror of this. Carole, now warming to her new-found role as mummy of the group, reassures them that she has scrubbed it out thoroughly. In that moment I catch Charley's eyes. They are narrowed and sly. She is chewing on the backs of her fingers, a sure sign with her that she is planning something. Or, in this case, has achieved it.

I sense what has happened. Charley, whose only conversation centres around her cousin who is a footballer, the clubs she goes to and the 'celebs' who court her company, is easy to dismiss as a loud-mouthed fool. She is but, dangerously, she also has flashes of pure genius. This is one of those. I guess she has told the others that I have pissed in the shower. The facts of the matter do not concern anyone. She has managed to select the one accusation most designed to pinpoint the other housemate's unformed judgement of me – she's old, therefore she wets herself – and, by chance has stumbled across a crime that might, just might, be unforgivable in my world. Right on with the first, wrong with the second.

The danger for me of Charley is uppermost in my mind. Goldstein is the enemy in 'Nineteen Eighty Four'. In this Big Brother it is the other contestants. There is already, and we have only been in each others company for a matter of hours, a code of behaviour that says that however badly someone behaves and however much they abuse you, you must speak and think well of them. So when, later, Charley behaves appallingly to us all, and to me directly in a typically insensitive way, I respond with, 'Are you stupid?' It is I who am put under great pressure from the others to apologise to her. I will not. She needs to be challenged. She can't be allowed to behave as she does and in any other circumstances but this – though I would never be in any other circumstances with this girl – I would be the one to do it.

My problem is that I do not know how the programme is being edited. I don't know how I am being perceived by the outside world or what the world makes of Charley. That she is becoming increasingly difficult to live with and the reasons for this may be invisible, for all I know, to the outside world. Above all there is a greater concern to me. The only series of Big Brother that I have watched is the Celebrity Big Brother shown earlier in the year. It featured the Shilpa Shetty and Jade Goody debacle. I followed the ensuing media discussions with a particular interest as a potential contestant. This, and the repeated warnings from the production team, makes me ultra-cautious. Charley, with her innate cunning, has already shown that she would use any weapon in her armoury as it comes to hand. It isn't always the most intelligent person who wins a battle. Sometimes the wisest thing is a dignified silence.

I encourage Shabs and Charley in their showgirl acts. Our suitcases have been delivered and they have all their clothes, which come at just the right psychological moment. They are changing every five minutes now and parading for themselves and each other. I enjoy this. It is at least something to watch and it keeps them from quarrelling which is increasing at an alarming rate. The knowledge that there are no boys, as they call them, has sunk in and they are disappointed and tetchy. They have convinced themselves that boys are being kept in another house and that the two shows are being broadcast simultaneously. They obsess that we are being set a task where if we find the key we shall have gained access to the other house. A sort of Da Vinci Code. The perceived wisdom is that this access will be through the pool. I think this is all rubbish but either I don't shout or I am too marginalized to be heard, but I think it worth making a positive suggestion.

My idea is based on a scene from The Poseidon Adventure. I am Shelley Winters. The fat non-swimming one. The ship goes down. A hole has to be made in the side of the pool, underwater, at the end where they think there is another pool, another house with the boys. The boys whom I suggest must be mute since they make no sound. Like Shelley I can be placed under water and shoved through the hole. Shelley and I have both proved we can swim underwater. Just an idea. Anything to get away from you lot.

There is a welcome file in the house which I have studied. It is not War and Peace but it is typed on paper and I am missing both. It contains a copy of the house rules as read to us all by the Cheeses plus a few instructions about household appliances. I have seen Tracey, the rule keeper, going through it but Carole has no need as She Knows Everything. The girls don't read it but Emily, who is the most distressed about no boys, is obsessive about the hunt for the imaginary key and is convinced that the Big Brother eye on the cover of the file is the key to unlocking the interconnecting door.

She would be better advised to read the contents of the file.

Chapter Eight

I am leading two quite separate lives within the house. In the first, I am self- absorbed and free to think and do as I like within the confines of my situation. So, normal, then. Just like real life. I have established a pattern of behaviour that which, if it were to be transferred to the outside world would not be regarded as anything particularly remarkable.

Each morning I wake and put on my microphone and, following Winston's example, I set my features in what I hope is an expression of quiet optimism. In the darkness, which is now familiar to me, I gather my clothes for the day and I take my wash things and go through to the bathroom. I creep and am silent so as not to disturb the girls. They have had no thought for me at four in the morning when they are screaming over nothing but consideration can be a one-way street. Later I will struggle into my day clothes under the duvet so as to be hidden from the cameras. This is an opportunity to test my newfound flexibility from the training sessions. We have been supplied with towels, which, along with the bed linen will be renewed each Thursday. From the communal pile each of us has taken two, one small, one medium. From what is left, which now lie scattered about the floor of the bedroom, I have taken one extra and have placed it under my mattress with the loo roll, the paper napkins, the cashew nuts and the bar of chocolate. In the night, at a moment of high tension between the girls, I call out 'Would anyone like a cashew nut?' I cannot tell you what they were quarrelling about because it is never clear what it is. What is certain is that it is a matter of no impor- tance but, like ill-parented toddlers, it goes on and on and just when you begin to think it might be subsiding it starts up again. Usually at four in the morning.

I have a fear of the shared towels. Not without reason. In particular I am haunted by the sight of Carole's soiled towel, which every day she drapes over the door of the warm cooker that is by my bed.

Alone in the bathroom in the glare of the twenty-four hour a day lighting I can almost relax. I have perfected my showering technique. While generally the house facilities are poor the shower is excellent. It is necessary for comfort to clean it out before use. The bathroom is covered with long, black hairs, some of them real hair, others hair extensions. They form a huge tidal wave that creeps from the bathroom, through the bedroom and threatens to engulf the sitting room. Shabs who, despite her self-obsession and delusions – 'I want to be bigger than Madonna' – I find curiously engaging, has some problem with her scalp which she scratches constantly. Perhaps one of the 'deals' that she might secure is with a scalp product company.

I am able, by wearing underwear and a thin dressing gown, to have more clothes on in the shower than in every day life. While I think it is unlikely that views of me in the shower will be a feature of prime time television I cannot know this for certain. There may be a peculiar taste that is more interested in me than the nubile beauties. I am leaving nothing to chance. I am determined, too, that I am not going to be the video entertainment at the production company's Christmas party.

I lay out my toiletries and makeup. Serried ranks, touching them, moving them, readjusting their positions, one day in order of use, another in size order. I am turning in to an obsessive. The other girls are leaving everything in piles, jumbled together on the bathroom shelves or on the floor. They don't share my sense of this is mine and that is yours. I have no experience of communal living.

I place a towel on the settee in the bathroom. All the seats in the house have ominous stains on them. Tracey adds –age to the end of her nouns. I described the foul little marks on the upholstery as 'seep-age', and she laughed with approval. I am learning.

I have learnt to slow each movement until it is a slow motion performance. I am Marcel Marceau. This is a unique experience for me. This filling of time. It is a lonely but not entirely unpleasant feeling. As I stand at the mirror moisturising my face I can sense a figure on the other side close to my face and I think I can hear his breathing.

The arrival of the suitcases was a huge relief. My now deep-seated paranoia made me afraid that they would be withheld and mentally I had prepared for this contingency.

I love my little corner of the bedroom. I can cope with the living conditions so long as no one touches my things. The rest of the room is filthy and chaotic with clothes and bits and shoes and makeup scattered everywhere. Like the bathroom it is impossible to know whose is whose and what is what in this jumble of tiny strips of fabric being trampled underfoot. There are some wonderful high-heeled shoes and if there is one thing I envy it is not the youth of the girls but their ability to walk confidently on these stilts. Perhaps it's the same thing.

I ask Charley if I might look at her Dolce and Gabbana leopard shoes. The suitcase inspectors have taken a flexible view of branding here. Charley loves money. She describes herself as a South East London It Girl which is an oxymoron. I think she knows the cost of It but not the value. She tells me that they cost nearly four hundred pounds. I'm not surprised. They are gorgeous. As indeed Charley can be. When she is not swearing, or bullying, or abusing, there are brief moments, just seconds when she has the face of a child angel. It is in that moment that I, who fears her most, love her and could see being in love with her. Give me my credit card. Let me, too, like the man Charley tells me bought her these shoes, rush off and buy her some Dolce and Gabbana's. I hope the omni-present camera catches **that** face, rarer than a panda's mating.

I am not in much of a position to take the moral high ground where Charley is concerned. Not only have I no idea what the boundaries are concerning pole and lap dancing, I am not entirely a stranger to a little body selling myself. In Portugal we owned huge swathes of land and a garden that ate up plants. In search of a source of cheap plants we found a small garden nursery near Faro. The Portuguese owner is literally a man of the soil. Extremely dirty and, sadly, just the type that is drawn to me. My Portuguese is academic rather than conversational which is a pity and he has no English but we have an unmistakeable shared language and common purpose. I want something from him as cheaply as possible and he wants something from me as cheaply as possible. As soon as he sees me he sees no need to hide his emotions and admiration. 'Amor,' he cries. 'Amor.' Much kissing and scraping of the skin on my face with his stubble. Hands everywhere. David, seeing the how the land lays and sensing a bargain, excuses himself and goes to the car. I am taken in to the gardener's little hut. I think briefly of Lady Chatterley. Negotiations begin. Much scraping of stubby piece of pencil on paper. More talk of 'amor'. Finally a price is agreed and we drive off with a boot full of plants, and more promised. The whole experience has been exhausting and grubby but well worth it. Though what I would have had to do for a pair of Dolce and Gabbana's doesn't bear thinking about.

It takes me just a few minutes to unpack. Despite the confiscation of my pink tissue paper, which grieves me when I think how the twins would have loved it, everything is immaculate. It is my bold ambition to keep it that way.

Carole will not be doing my washing. I have watched as each day, all day and into the night, she pounds clothes in the bath in the sitting room. Just now she has come from the diary room crying. We sit at the dining table, just the two of us, and I probe without prying. It is one of the girl's rules of engagement to ask each other and me constantly 'Are you all right?' They walk away instantly. They don't want an answer but just feel they are doing their duty by seeming to care. This looks serious and I want an answer. She tells me that she has just been told that her son, whose age I can't quite catch but I gather is young, has been sectioned.

My first thought, I confess, is of Virginia Woolf who, like Carole, was a socialist, though I would struggle to find any other similarity. I think of her fits of madness and of Mrs Dalloway and wonder how they would both have coped here. I think of how Virginia has been stolen from us by Hollywood, as they have done with Austen, Shakespeare and the D-day landings. They have taken Virginia's books and given them daft notes of explanation, as though it were possible to explain anyone, any place, any time so English to an American, and have claimed her through the cinema as their own. In an attempt at fairness I have to say that this stealing of literature and history when all you have is Huckleberry Finn and Starbucks is fairly understandable. I feel a tad guilty about drifting off while Carole's motherly heart is breaking but she is very anti-war and therefore anti-American so would probably agree with me.

I am uncertain if the young man in question is her son or foster son. I have tried to unravel the family tree of her relationships but it is early days and it is all rather complex. With the arrival of our suitcases and clothes came other items that have been revealing. The girls and I have different ideas of what constitutes 'basics' and the Packing Inspectors have been generous to them, in my opinion. When I see what they have brought in I am beginning to regret my early written declaration, made in those far off days in Cardiff, that I wanted George Clooney, my husband and a Fortnum's hamper as my luxuries. That was when I thought it was a game. Silly me. However, there is still time.

The twins have brought a suitcase of pink and Laura has a huge leopard print dressing gown that she proceeds to wear day and night. Tracey, like me, swiftly and privately secretes her clothes in to a couple of drawers. No mess-age there then. Chanelle, who is the age of a grown woman to me, is re-united with Betsy, a rather disgusting floppy toy which I gather is a rabbit. I know it is unfair to judge on first meeting but I hate

Betsy. Perhaps Chanelle, innocent looking, always ever so slightly poorly, with pretensions to Posh, will turn out to be a bunny boiler.

Other housemates have brought photographs from home. The contract with the production company states that the rights to the photographs will from that time rest with their company. I wouldn't in any case have taken photographs with me. It is hard enough to be away from my family as it is without having photographs with me and I am unlikely to forget what they look like. Other people's photographs are another matter. I love them. I am not in the least interest in holiday snaps. If I want to see what somewhere looks like I will go myself, but a wedding album of complete strangers is my idea of heaven. Seeing these housemates' relatives and friends makes me aware of their bigger picture. It is a story of single parenting, divorce, happy marriage, black and white and all shades in between and, the case of the twins, pink friends. I can see that each of these people, these outsiders, has a story to tell and possibly sell. I wish I could meet them. They could call in to the house and have tea with us. It would make for jolly television. And then I remember that, along with everything else that is missing from a decently run house, we don't have a tea-pot.

As well as being the oldest person ever to have entered the Big Brother house – putting aside Celebrity Big Brother – I am the only one here who has left behind a long-term relationship. A husband even. It will be interesting to see which of those two peculiarities proves to be the ultimate deal-breaker.

So, when Carole tells me about the incarceration of her son I am uncertain about the finer points of their relationship. I feel for her. It must be absolutely dreadful and, to be stuck in this place, hearing that must be nigh on impossible. It is one of the cruel ironies of life that when she came in to the house she said that part of her motivation was to find out for herself what prison life was like as she had worked with young offenders. I shall go with her to help pack her case. Case packing is an emotive activity in this house. I remember Shilpa Shetty saying it was the endless case packing that got her down, which was saying something in the face of stiff opposition from Jade and her mother in the stress stakes.

There turns out to be no case packing. Carole wipes her eyes and nose on the candlewick nightie that she wears night and day, and returns to the bath where clothes' soaking awaits her.

Later I am concerned for Carole. Nothing is ever said to me again or in my hearing about the boy but it is clear that Carole is not happy and I would like to be supportive. In this place we go from being total strangers to an intensity of emotional intimacy that is frightening in its speed in the face of a real ignorance about each other. There is no background knowledge to help paint a fuller picture. I guess it is like being a Samaritan except we are all the clients. Plus we can't trust each other.

It is very difficult for me to keep to my decision not to talk about family. This decision is based on the principle that it is I, not they, who have chosen to forgo my privacy and enter this alien world. I am, and always have been, an independent woman. To the question 'Who are you?' wife and mother would not be the first words that come to mind. I am surprised, therefore, to find how much I would speak about them if I could and how limiting it is having them out of bounds. I refer to them constantly in my thoughts. When I occasionally make some reference to my past or to my home-life, because of this self-imposed censorship, it comes out all stilted and I feel like I am showing off. Porsche. Staff. Harvey Nichols. Houses. I don't like it.

The common factors between us of Big Brother auditions and pre-event incarceration are not allowed to be discussed, which rules out a useful tool of shared experience in building relationships. We are not allowed, either, to talk about previous contestants or programmes. Worse, we can't bitch about the production team, a fertile ground for chat, and something from which we could create a common enemy which would bring us all together. I am surprised now how deferential and unquestioning they are towards Big Brother.

For all their bravado, aggression and name-calling I think that I am the rebel here.

Carole is in the garden at the mangle. I am happy that she has largely taken this job from me. I can see why the mangle is now virtually obsolete and why James Dyson has not chosen to refine it as he did with the vacuum cleaner. It takes a garment, drags it through its rollers, squeezing the life out its fabric, breaking all buttons and distorting the zip so it never works again, and impregnating it with wood chips. It is so busy doing this that it forgets its primary function of removing water.

The clothes washing programme is, in Tracey's words, 'doing my head in'. Carole shouts at people for not handing her their washing and then it lies intermingling in a heap in the corner of the sitting area. She fills the bath with water and washing powder and throws everything, everything, in together. She then pummels some more, soaks, and pummels. The water takes on the consistency and colour of mud.

Once the clothes have been truly murdered, they are draped over garden furniture, or on the backs of chairs or any other surface to fester.

I remember river cruises down the Nile. Wonderful happy holidays that lulled me into thinking I could function in a group. I promise myself that I will go again.

I have travelled the world, spent months in the deepest parts of Africa, travelled throughout India, eating everything on offer, turning up my nose at nothing and have never once had a stomach upset. I don't intend to start now. I would sooner drink a gallon of water from the infected river of the Nile than let Carole wash my clothes. As for the food...

While Carole is out of the way sobbing over her self-imposed workload, I ask the housemates if I might have a word. Charley looks at me much as to say, 'You still here?' She walks away with Shabs in tow. I tell them that I am worried about Carole. Do you remember Mrs Dale and her diary on the wireless, as it was called then? Her catchphrase, though it wasn't called that then, was, 'I'm worried about Jim,' her doctor husband. I'm worried about Carole. I tell them that Carole is doing unnecessary washing. She takes clothes that are barely worn and gives herself work. I say that she doesn't seem happy and perhaps we can help. I have talked with her, I say, and she has so many interesting aspects to her life, perhaps we can encourage her to tell us about them. I am aware that I sound patronising but it is that or staying mute for thirteen weeks.

I don't know whether anything will happen as a result but imagine that the twins and Nicky, at least, will respond to this.

George Elliot stated that the whole purpose of art and literature is to perceive imaginatively why others feel differently from ourselves. Just when I think that there is nothing left in the world untouched by the artist and wordsmith, that everything past and present has been chewed over, digested and spat out, time and time again, then someone comes along who defies analysis. I would challenge any artist or writer, dead or alive, to explain what the twins think or feel. Except about pink, of course. I am on a mission to find out.

I am certain that the twins are kind. Kind. It is a trivial little word in itself but there is too little kindness in the world and it has become a rare commodity. When I was imprisoned in the hotel in North Wales I had to paint a mug, I inscribed the words 'Be Kind' round the edge.

In terms of the game we are playing, if we remember that it is a game, I think the twins, despite the outward silliness of them, are the ones to most fear. They are the most capable of denouncing you to the Thought Police and the most likely to be heard. They are going to win this. Deffo.

I have invented a little game to amuse myself. Using a pink cup as a microphone I 'interview' housemates. Talking to the twins, individually, in this way was intriguing. Most of us are layers with different strands of personality, good, bad, kind, cruel, a good old mixture. I am an onion. Peel off the layers and I might make you cry. With the twins it is a rare case of what you see is what you get. They are deep down pink. I ask about their studies. They have just finished the first year of a degree course in social work at university. Amanda tells me about the papers they have submitted on 'gratification'. I perk at this. 'That seems to be relevant to our situation here, don't you think?' I have nearly lost her but the pink microphone gives the necessary authority to press on. It is a stroke of genius on my part. 'What can you tell us about immediate gratification?' Not a lot, it seems. Deferred gratification? No. I quite wonder what their papers were about. It is a very useful exercise, however, because I do learn about the differences between them, which they are open to talk about. While it is their choice to be seen as one unit they have differing ideas and plans. One is keen to continue with the degree course, the other is drawn to 'fashion'. Despite the fluffiness they are tough as old boots and canny with it. Which doesn't stop me from being concerned about them.

When I analyse this I think of an example. The other girls routinely swear. Emily in particular has the dirtiest language, especially after dark. This doesn't rub off on me. No one would expect it to. Why should the twins pick this up? They don't.

I know that Nicky will have heard what I have said about Carole. We have talked, and she has told me the story of her birth in India and her adoption by English parents with its involvement of Mother Theresa of Calcutta. I feel pleased that she should chose to go further and tell me what feel like confidences, although I know there is a wider audience beyond the cameras. I admire her for taking the risk of coming on this programme which has involved her giving up her safe job. I also like the sound of her Auntie, with whom she is close and should take some of the responsibility for Nicky's high standards in domestic matters. A girl after my own heart. In the highly unlikely event that Nicky becomes desperate for a job she can come and be my housekeeper. She isn't going to get much chance to cook here – Carole will see to that – but give her a few decent ingredients and she can produce food that I like. She cooks, she cleans, she's beautiful, she is passionate, and she's intelligent. Let me out of here so I can find her a husband. Except she hates men. Half the world's population is hateful.

Love is for losers. She shows me her stuffed toy dinosaur. A previous boyfriend cut off his head. I accept that she can be infuriating. When she shows me two tops and asks for my help in choosing which one to wear I deliberate and point to one. 'How horrible do I look in the other one?' She won't let it go. The glass is half empty. She says that when she is around me she doesn't swear so much. I have some function, then, and not a bad one at that.

Nicky will assume that Carole has a compulsive cleaning disorder but, if Nicky talking with her, gets Carole away from that ruddy mangle and bath I shall feel I haven't lived in vain.

All this tension is carried out against the backdrop of Charley and Shabs screaming. Emily is the third cohort and this subordinate role doesn't sit easily with her. Her chance to show us her 'performing arts skills' of which she speaks so highly is coming shortly. We are given our first task.

I think I will go and sit in the bathroom for a while to see if Charles Dickens or Wilkie Collins would like to have a chat with me.

Chapter Nine

In 'Nineteen Eight Four' there is a prediction, considered extraordinary at the time of its publication, that by the year 2050 Chaucer, Shakespeare, Milton and Byron would have been destroyed. Absolutely preposterous. Big Brother contestants, aided and abetted by modern education, which reflects the paucity of society's values, has done this in 2007.

In the place of a complex, rich and sometimes opaque dictionary from which to express ourselves we are driven out of fear to an assassination of language. Tracey, and to varying degrees all the others, have created their own Newspeak which takes the place of traditional English. This new language is composed of short, clipped words and sayings repeated over and over again.

Big Brother has shown its genius in the choice of Tracey as housemate. She beautifully personifies Orwell's perception of an Oceanian resident. 'ave it... 'ave it in a field...gravy...get over it...it's doing my 'ed in...sketchy...Even the adding of the suffix –age to nouns is pure Newspeak. At first I thought Tracey was in on the joke, a 'plant' perhaps, but as I get to know her a little better – it is never possible to know Tracey – I can see that her speech is a genuine incarnation of all that Orwell had in mind. Her words, her limited, repetitive vocabulary uniquely evokes no memories in my mind. They neither remind me of anything nor do they set me off on some independent thought. They never inspire. It is as though they are designed to wipe out thought and with it creativity, individuality and any thought of true friendship. They are not the words of a true rebel.

The pink hair, the multi-coloured jacket, her hobby of collecting string and her carrier bag collection, her roll-your-own cigarettes are not subversive but conventional. Her neatness, her rule observing, her impatience with my unhappiness are all expressions of her conformity. I wonder if it were ever thus. Tracey will win this. Deffo.

The twins, too, are pure Newspeak. They are incapable of heretical thought and their language with its studied limited vocabulary reflects this. They gabble and the sound is both high-pitched and monotonous. For both the twins and Tracey speech has become independent of consciousness, a sort of reflex action to fill a necessary void.

Charley, too, has a series of phrases fired out loudly and monotonously, as though from a machine gun. 'I ain't bovvered..I ain't lying...on my muvvers life..' interspersed by her favourite and most used word, fuck.

My own language, by comparison, is, predictably, 'old think', with its larger vocabulary and its ability to be objective and rational. Let me be clear here, I'm talking about the vocabulary, not the user of it. As I speak it sounds archaic and rather decadent. As though I am taking the piss. Which I am some of the time, just falling back on my humour to keep me going. My way of speaking sadly alienates me further from them but, just as I find their language foreign, I can't latch on to their humour. They talk about 'aving a laugh but it's not as I know it. I shouldn't think they watch television comedy even mainstream stuff like Little Britain. My favourite Spike Milligan would terrify them. Whatever their sense of humour they don't appear to be having any fun here.

Just as in Oceania, expressing opinions above a very low, basic level or having what is thought of as a conversation in the world I know is virtually impossible. I try. I really do try.

Nicky and I speak about relationships. She is having an endless struggle with herself to unravel her feelings about men. She claims to hate men, to see them all as users, but from watching her interact with the others I think that, like me, she isn't a girls' girl. She is feminine, more so than most of the others, and part of that conventional femininity wants to be married. Later, when she mutters 'marry me' it is not to anyone in particular but to the world of men at large. It seems to me to be a simple case of not having met the right man. Get out there and keep kissing frogs. I am not by nature an advice giver but adopting an auntie role, as I know she is missing hers terribly, I advise her to have more confidence and relax more. Nothing is going to frighten off a man more than her intensity.

Chanelle has paid me two verbal compliments. She laughs, rather uncertainly, but still she laughs at my 'jokes'. Then she looked at me, probably the only person in the house to have looked at me, and says, 'When I get to your age I hope I'm like you.' Not look like you, but the greater compliment of being like me. She can be a sweet girl. She is embarrassed by what she has said so I say, 'If you are blessed!'

We are seated in the living area and it strikes me that I can bear the cruelty and insecurity of life in the house more easily than its bareness and its listlessness. There is a lull in the screaming and quarrelling and I venture a little story. My conceit is that I may occasionally be able to engage with a tiny anecdote, to connect or interest. Such vanity.

They have been talking about clubs and boys. It is an identical conversation that is repeated, mantra-like, day in, day out on an endless loop. Charley and her 'celebs'. Footballers. 'Celebs'. I don't know the names she drops. It doesn't look as though the other girls do either, but she enthrals them. The sheer repetition, the shouting, 'celebs, celebs' is now a chant in their blood. The names I must never drop wouldn't in any case impress them. What would? Poor old Portugal could only boast Clive Dunn and Cliff Richard, sad, though Gloucestershire can boast its fair share of A-listers. Coming down the alphabet I think of Laurence Llewelyn-Bowen. Perhaps not. I don't think in my entire life I have met anyone who has been to Chinawhites.

I tell them that I have not been without my admirers and am not a stranger to the pick-up line. Just a few years ago David and I were dining in a favourite restaurant near Shepherds Market. David engages with his food. He doesn't just eat it. As well as appreciating its taste and smell he is much concerned with its look. Not just the first impression when the lid is lifted or the plate placed in front of you, but its look throughout the whole meal. It must be 'composed', moved about. While this could be annoying it leaves me free to chat on. We are not a married couple who sit in silence over a meal. We engage and entertain each other.

On this occasion I was vaguely aware of a large couple, probably Germans, across the room engaged in a more typical marital non-conversation. At the end of the meal David excused himself to wash his hands and the German gentleman seized the moment to leap to his feet and march to our table. Bowing his head and clicking his heels, re-enforcing national stereotyping, he said, 'Madam, here is my card. There will always be a bed for you in Dusseldorf.' With that he marched back to his silent wife. I have kept the card just in case.

This modest conversational offering lies on the plastic coffee table in front of us along with the used pieces of cotton wool, nail polishes, eyebrow pluckers, and all the other detritus that goes towards being girlie. Finally Chanelle, who might have been thinking about this and is a polite girl, asks genuinely, 'Who is Dusseldorf?' Not where, but who.

I should have known better. I feel, and am, a fool. If I am to chat I shall in future confine my conversations to Charles, Gertrude and Wilkie. Here I shall confide a secret. I have a tiny glimmer of hope that will not be extinguished like a Toc H lamp. Big Brother might yet send me a little friend.

Later, against all my best instincts I try again. My interest in Victorian writers occasionally allows me to give talks to literary groups and book clubs and the like. Because some who attend might never have enjoyed the people I speak about, having had it spoilt for them at school, I put those Victorian lives in to a modern context. I simply explore the view that nothing changes. For example, I make the very obvious link between Dickens and David Beckham. The cult of celebrity, the product endorsements, the obsessive disorders, public ridicule – it's all there. It seems to me that Chanelle with her encyclopaedic knowledge of the Beckhams might be interested in the link I make. It would also benefit me to learn from her. I have read their autobiographies and various books about them to help me establish my links but she will know a lot that I don't. Do bear in mind that there are hours on end, even days, when nothing happens in the house. I do not wish to teach, more likely learn.

Briefly, I tell her about my interest and say I would like to ask her a question that she may be able to help with. Dickens suffered much ridicule, like David. One example surrounds his love of geraniums, also a favourite of mine, but which then and now can be seen as a vulgar plant and municipal. Dickens and I don't give a toss. I ask about the Beckhams favourite flowers. For just a second she is intrigued, as much by the fact that she doesn't know and she resolves on being 'released' to find out. I want to tell her about Dickens love of mirrors inspired by his pride in his beautiful long brown hair and how he set hair fashions for young men when he was in his twenties. But she is called back, dragged back by the invisible cord of the pack, to the group of girls basking in the sun. 'Celebs'. They talk about pink and speculate pointlessly about the existence of boys over the wall. It would never occur to them that I might need 'boys', or rather a man, too.

I acknowledge to myself what they see. I am old. I wish I could oblige them and it be otherwise. The Lesley of forty years ago would wipe the floor with them. The Lesley, who isn't painfully aware of the all-judging eye of the camera, would also wipe the floor with them. I am also a bore. Worse, I am like a teacher. A group of people who, if I generalise, I loath. I am guilty of what Orwell calls 'duck speak' which when applied to an opponent is a term of abuse and when applied to someone you agree with is praise. I'm quacking.

The twins and Charley and Shabs have gone inside to change their bikinis for the tenth time that day. They jump on the furniture. I tried it once here, running from sofa to sofa, round as round as they do, to see if it felt dangerous, naughty, wild. It just felt pointless. I was deafened by the sound of my mother, again, turning in her non-existent grave. She's been doing a lot of that recently.

I can't in any case at my age afford to break a hip.

The excitement of our first task!

We are to engage in a break dancing competition. We are shown a demonstration on video, given individual outfits to wear and instructions to divide into two teams to practice. We shall be competing later on an improvised stage in the sitting room. Tasks it seems are few and far between. It would be fair to assume that my experience of break dancing is limited, to nil, and I don't really know what it is. However, I am so bored that if they said the task was to hack off my own leg with a teaspoon I would be digging in to the very flesh.

Teams are chosen. No one wants me. I wouldn't want me. Emily doesn't bother to hide her contempt and horror at being landed with me. I respect her for that. She is right. I put up a miserable show but what she doesn't know is that I am always on life's winning team. Rivalry is fierce and Emily, our leader, with a lifetime of experience as an actress and performer she tells us, proves to be an impatient teacher. Her support and instruction to me is confined to a curled lip and clipped, 'Do you know what a teddy bear roll is?' 'Of course I don't know what a teddy bear roll is. I'm sixty years old.' What I don't tell her is that I would never have been able to break dance and would never have been interested. The divide between us, Emily, is not of age.

Emily is a conundrum.

She is a pretty girl, not attractive to my eye with her sulky mouth and false pretensions, but I can see that if the amateur dramatics want a female Prince Charming for the pantomime then she would be ideal. She would be more attractive if she were less confident of her all encompassing talents. She does have moments of unintentional humour and I like her for that. She asks me, 'Are those earrings from the olden days?' Sensitively she enquires of the twins, 'Being twins, if one of you dies, does the other one die too?' She is engaged in a fierce competitive battle to ally herself with Charley and Shabs. She is a brave girl. She also has the guts to try to take me on. She suspects that I don't like her and she has good reason to dislike me. She aspires to present herself as the spoilt, pampered favourite daughter of a wealthy family. Her cheap and shabby wardrobe, inferior to the other girls, lends the lie to this. I don't know or care about the truth of the matter. We are all entitled to play a game. What irritates me is that her performance, for an actress of her self-declared genius, is unconvincing. We engage in the occasional verbal sparring match. Surprisingly, I am encouraged in this by Tracey, with whom I have formed what to the casual onlooker would be an unlikely alliance.

As we practice for the dance contest Emily has adopted a sort of American street voice. I think that is what it is. At times her vocabulary, as well as her table manners, makes me think that in a previous life she was a stevedore in the docks of Bristol, her hometown, that she describes as being in Gloucestershire. She wants a foot in all camps as she professes that she is 'street' and, after dark in particular, she resorts to obscenities that don't sit comfortably with such a pretty face. I am suspicious that she is not as street-wise as she thinks. But the girl has courage. There is no doubt of that.

Charley, meanwhile, who is always driven by discontent, is focussing her anger on the outfit that Big Brother has supplied. I like it as it is all encompassing but these are the grounds of Charley's objections. She is riddled with petty grievance and sees the world as being full of carefully designed slights aimed specifically at her.

I am disappointed. I had hoped a task, and especially one so close to the girl's talents and interests would perk us up a bit. Not so. The usual bickering, discontents, and jealousies rule the day and it is a miserable affair. Only Carole throws herself in to it and she is brilliant. Absolutely brilliant. She gets my award for being game. Though perhaps I should revise that word which, from where I come, means something you shoot and it hangs about for a long time until it becomes smelly. Well, why not?

The practising and the competition, which will presumably be shown on prime television, take up the whole day. While I can only fairly be judged the worst individual at break dancing I have been right in my prediction. I am on the winning team. Emily, who is good at break dancing but hopeless at teamwork, is judged best. Her triumph is a relief to us all.

I think of Sharon Osbourne's father, Don Arden, who was a contemporary of David's. He was one of the most famous managers of rock groups until Sharon eclipsed him in the fame firmament. In the sixties a rival manager, Robert Stigwood, tried to lure away one of Arden's groups. Arden went to Stigwood's office, lifted him from his chair, dragged him to the balcony and threatened to throw him over. Stigwood, Arden recalled, 'never bothered me again.'

Emily will never be a manager of people and I am considering taking her to the balcony and throwing her over, metaphorically speaking.

After the task Laura falls back into her bed from which she is becoming reluctant to leave. She sits there, Buddha-like, in her leopard print dressing gown pronouncing on matters. She is beginning to remind me of one of those television programmes where Americans have become so fat they have to have the side taken off their house when they need to go to hospital. On her first evening she described herself as being narrow-minded and that she wanted to broaden her experience by meeting people through this programme. I have been fascinated to see how since coming through that fatal entrance door each of us has faded, but no one more than Laura. She would like to cook but Carole and Nicky have engaged in battle over the kitchen and she has retired, beaten. Of all of us she is the one with the least energy and purpose except, frighteningly, her ability to pontificate. She reminds me of Scott of the Antarctica, for no good reason, and I am Captain Oates.

During this time I have been struggling to convince Shabs that she shouldn't leave. Obsessed by 'deals' she asks constantly if these would be at risk if she left so soon. She has been talking about this since day one. I go to great lengths, using every persuasive skill at my command, to get her to stay. Shabs has enormous personal energy but my thought is that this is unlikely to be well channelled in the workplace. She confirms this. She never stays in a job more than four or five days. The fact that she tells me about this so often and tells me about her ex-teacher who has been in touch to express concern for her, alerts me that she might be seeking some affirmation from me. I am drawn to her. I advise her that this Big Brother experience is one from which she should not withdraw. 'Let them evict you. Do not walk.' I tell her, 'Let this be a turning point. An occasion when you stick something out. An important opportunity for not being a quitter.'

This is sound advice. While I like her and she would be good television I think the others will feel that she is expendable. Her alliance with Charley, although inevitable, will do her no favours. She is not going to be here for long in any case. I tell her that 'deals' would be most compromised by her 'walking'. 'Walkers' are the most despised of all the housemates. The public believes that they have wasted a place, taken theirs, even. This is rubbish as there are others waiting in the wings throughout the run of the show to take our places. Go out evicted and you are a winner. Go out a walker and you are a loser for life. She takes this on board but it is an ongoing battle and I need to keep an eye on her. The others, those who want to win and those who are too selfish to think beyond the minute, would prefer her to go.

My own more urgent consideration is that if anyone 'walks', Shabs, it is going to be me. If Shabs walks the production team is going to be less likely to let me go. Stay, Shabs, stay.

The girls are spending more and more time in bed turning the days into night and nights into fights. Carole is at the bath washing things. I remember an article I read about the menopause. One of the benefits of the menopause, it says, is that women often become leaders in their community, valued and respected for their wisdom and knowledge. Just then Carole's three-day-old bean juice encrusted candlewick-clad bosom swings among the washing as it does with the food she cooks. Heaven help us if the article is true.

I sit in the garden. I deserve a bit of 'me time' after my unrewarding social work. Gertrude isn't needy. She is like me. She just wants to get away.

My mind turns morbidly to funerals again, the ultimate getting away from it all.

I have an unsatisfactory relationship with God at the best of times and the last few days of my life have done nothing to improve it. There are no 'believers' here, though Nicky is a Catholic, and I am disappointed. I had rather hoped there would be a Born Again Something Or Another. They could have sorted me out in this respect at least. I am one of the few people in the world who would welcome being incarcerated with a Christian – though I would draw the line at Terry Waite, of course.

The funeral that engages my morbid thoughts this time took place in Portugal. There is just the one small Church of England building in the Algarve, privately built by a generous English benefactress. It is a pretty, white washed concoction with bell tower situated in the grounds of a nursing home and old people's village. Its major virtue lies in its proximity to the regular trade both in life and death that the elderly brings to it. In our search for a few answers to the God-question David and I are members of the congregation on the understanding that we are intellectually and spiritually curious rather than committed. Which is more than can be said for the rest of the congregation or indeed the unlikely person God has chosen to lead the flock. I do have a reputation in the family of being a person who starts at the top of any organisation and works her way down. In this case I am on the church council without benefit of confirmation or belief. It is a bit like post-modern irony. Someone has to do it and it could be seen as one in the same thing.

An elderly lady has died and the funeral is being planned. Her husband, who is a bit of a bully and fantasist, has written a eulogy for her. Towards the End she was a manky old thing and it was a blessing when she went and I am surprised when I hear that there is antagonism about anyone from the congregation reading this at the funeral. I am not good at public speaking but I like doing it. Being a clean and fresh little girl with formidable parents I was always the orator for school plays and the like including the all important nativity play. My mother awaited the allocation of this role each year with complete confidence. She gave me a piece of advice that has seen me in good stead through the years. 'Never get involved with a man who was a shepherd in the school nativity play.' Try it; it's always worked for me.

I ask to see the eulogy and see what the fuss is about. Mr B., the grieving widower, has given vent to his fantasy side. Mrs B. has done everything in her life. She has won Wimbledon, twice, has been a world famous vet, has climbed Kilimanjaro alone, and recently saved a Royal baby as it fell from a yacht off the coast of Greece. None of this knits with our memory of Mrs B. But heck, who are we to judge when each week we are asked to vouch for a virgin birth and stones being rolled away from caves? I will read the eulogy.

I am a brave woman to stand before the congregation and read aloud that a Doctor Barnard assisted Mrs B. when she performed the world's first heart transplant. There is a tiny audience. Just the Chaplain, the man who proves that if God exists He has a sense of humour, Mr B., the grieving widower who looks as though he is relishing his moment in the spotlight and a few people from the nursing home who, looking at the state of them, shouldn't bother going home. And me. In that place I have decided not to wear black. There are so many deaths it would look as though you were too lazy to change between funerals.

Mrs B. herself is there in a pale wooden coffin draped with a flag like Lord Louis Mountbatten, except this flag is of the Isle of Man where Mrs B. spent a very happy holiday one summer.

The Chaplain has brought along a tape recorder and presses a button. An unfamiliar and not very pleasing dirge issues forth and God's apprentice says it is the Isle of Man anthem. The tape, predictably, breaks and he says we are to sing along alone to the end. Unfamiliar with the said anthem I sing instead Swing Low Sweet Chariot without benefit of knowledge of tune or words. It all passes off as well as can be expected and, most importantly, Mr B. is happy, which to my mind is the point of the exercise.

As we prepare to leave the church I stop for a moment to look at Mrs B.'s coffin. There is a small round table next to it covered in a pretty floral tablecloth. Mr B. has placed on it a vase of apricot-coloured roses which he tells me were Mrs B.'s favourites. I am moved, as one should be at a funeral. Next to the roses is a framed photograph. I lean closer to take a look. Perhaps I will glean clues about the younger Mrs B., the all-capable world leader. In the frame is the photograph that came with it when Mr B. bought it. It is of Claudia Schiffer.

My reveries about God and his existence are interrupted by Big Brother. We gather in the sitting room. It is Friday night, usually eviction night, and wild speculation is rife among housemates.

The loud speakers in the house play the sound of crowds screaming. There is an echo outside in the real world. I am still half contemplating the existence of God when the doors open. Someone has had their prayers answered. In walks a shiny, glossy, gorgeous vision, brimming with self-confidence and charisma. 'A stripper', says Laura.

Thank you, God. It's Ziggy.

CHAPTER TEN

The relief on seeing Ziggy floods over me. While aware that, as we say in my family, no good will come of it, at least it will give the girls something to play with. It does, however, smack of putting one toy in the playpen for six children to fight over.

He has good manners and greets me with a respectful cheek kiss. He and I will be all right. My relief is tinged with disappointment. While it would have been unreasonable to expect Andrew Marr to drop everything to be at my side I had hoped that Big Brother would see what a joke it would be to send in a little gift for me, too. It wouldn't have been difficult. My taste in men is eclectic. At least in the short term. But probably excludes anyone who would come in to the Big Brother house.

The girls, meanwhile, have no concept of hospitality. They crowd and scream and do their set pieces but make no effort to sensibly orientate our newcomer. I go to the Diary Room and ask for alcohol, the only sane response to having a guest.

That night there is much discussion as to where Ziggy is to sleep. He is not bothered but would like a decision. The only person in this place capable of making any sort of sensible decision buries her head in her glass of wine. I am not prepared to give up my bed. I know there are rumblings about this, especially from Tracey who it really doesn't concern at all, but I choose to be deaf. If they have the guts to challenge me face to face then I shall staunchly defend my corner. If that fails and they take my bed by force, which is what would be required, then Plan B is that I should sleep in the bathroom. The sofa there is comfortable and I am so tired that the all-night lighting would be no problem. I become pivotal in what happens and how events unfold.

The sexual hysteria that has enveloped the house now has a focus on Ziggy and the next few days become a battleground. The girls' interest in him does not extend to getting up earlier in the morning and they keep to their near afternoon rising. I am the first to rise, as ever, and my morning ritual continues quite happily.

Each morning I take out all my clothes from the drawers and shake and refold them and lay them neatly on the bed. Once a girl asks me why I do this and I explain that it refreshes them. It is a simple, satisfying bonding experience. The clothes carry with them a slight smell and memory of home and of a better life. I do not say that this morning ritual is planned to be seen so that when I do it for the last time it will come as no surprise to the others. I am interested to see that Ziggy, who watches everything, adopts this technique. He, like me, has shopped especially for this experience. He has a pair of linen trousers that remind me of David. I tell him this. He likes to keep order amongst his possessions and is often infuriated by the chaos around him. He shows me the photographs of his family and I particularly bond with his mother with whom, on the basis of a grainy snap, I feel a lot in common. A woman with standards, I should think. But Ziggy's love and pride lies in Molly, his dog, and he becomes a little moist about the eyes as he talks about her. Molly will be a hard act to follow.

It is some testament to Ziggy's good manners and sensitivity that I am comfortable when he joins me in the mornings in the bathroom. I continue unselfconsciously with my daft little rituals in front of him. We talk about his previous relationships and he speaks of the usual difficulties and breakings up but is always gallant about ex-girlfriends. I ask what he looks for in a girlfriend and he talks about energy and competence and get up and go. I think his definition of attractive and mine is similar. I like the way, too, that he talks about his sport. Unlike most 'blokes' he doesn't show off or exaggerate. He was a decent tennis player but when I ask if he thought of taking it further, professional tennis was a possibility, he laughs at himself and says he was too concerned with how he looked and how many rackets he had. When we speak about golf, which is one of my great loves, and of golf courses he isn't denigrating or patronising which is unusual in such a conversation. I tell him I am cunning around the greens which should tell him about me if he is interested. We talk a little about the boy band of which he was a member but neither of us is much interested in that. I am comfortable with him and learn more about him in our morning chats than I will ever know about the girls. Why can't they talk in this way? They don't even do it among themselves.

We have our second house meeting. I propose it as an opportunity for each of us to express how we feel and to air any problems. The atmosphere cannot be worse. I am wrong. I adopt the conch shell principle, which I think they may be familiar with, thinking they will have read Lord of the Flies at school. I am trying to be gently guiding, rather than assertive, conscious of the final end to Piggy in the book.

I pick up a banana and in an attempt to keep some order pass it around. You can speak when you have the banana. At other times you must be quiet. Some understand, most see this as an unwelcome interruption of their chaotic grumbling. When it comes to my turn I say that, while it is not a concern of mine, what has surprised me is that the girls express a desire to have careers in the spotlight, in entertainment or the media stemming from this experience, but they are making nothing of what seems to me to be a wonderful opportunity to show off their talents. It is a thirteen-week audition. If anyone were to be offered five minutes on television they would jump at the chance and here they have an audience of millions for as long as they like. It continues to amaze me that anyone would be watching. I pass the banana to the next person.

I show from this that I have absolutely no idea what the programme is about or what is the nature of this new 'celebrity'.

I am never to recover from what I have said. All the unspoken resentments about me are to be shared now in heated talk about me in the garden and the bedroom. One of the characteristics of the house is that it is believed that you can simply move to another area and not be heard or that I am unable to know by knowledge and instinct what will be said. I can see by her body language that Tracey, in particular, is furious. I hear Emily, of all people, defending me. 'She didn't mean anything by it,' she says. I wish one of them would challenge me. I am a non-confrontational person who this evening wants to be provoked. I want to tell them how much they, in their words, piss me off.

I go to see Big Brother in the Diary Room. I have thought about what I will say. I speak slowly, firmly, with deliberation, as though speaking to an idiot. There is to be no mistake about my meaning or my intent. I am going to leave. I say, 'I am more bored than is acceptable to me.' With a carefully contrived gesture that I judge will convince the psychologists I move my hands forward and pull them back towards myself and say, 'I will be withdrawing.' As expected, the team point how briefly I have been in the house. They say people usually change their minds. I don't engage in much conversation but do express concern about how I am being seen by the wider audience. I guess that I will be seen simply as an old snob sitting in the corner being judgemental. This is not how I am or wish to be seen. On top of that I am not having fun or being fun. We agree that I shall think about it and return in two days to speak further. I have given warning and through the camera I have given warning to David, if it is transmitted, and I leave it at that. I am not to know that events will overtake me that will cause me to have to delay my departure.

As I leave the Diary Room I am aware that I have been away from the house for a long time. Charley and Shabs lurk at the door. I know they cannot hear what has been said and that they always have a slightly guilty air about them. It is, however, one of Charley's defining characteristics that she has no conscience.

I say, 'don't worry about me. I won't be here much longer.' The effect is hilarious. Shabs, in her delightfully dramatic way, takes this to mean that I have a terminal illness. She whispers this to Charley and they collapse, hugging each other convulsed in tears and misery. Then they hug and cry over me. I don't enjoy all the touching and kissing and mauling that is a feature of the house. It smacks of hypocrisy.

We have all read of revenges that ex-wives perpetrate on errant husbands. Giving away their best wine cellar to strangers, cutting off the end of all his ties, that sort of thing. My personal favourite is placing frozen prawns in the hem of the curtains. The stench becomes intolerable over the months and permeates everywhere so that its source is undetectable. I plan some revenge in my mind. Though we have neither prawns nor curtains.

The battle over Ziggy is fierce. Interestingly, Charley is not interested in him for herself, as she wants a ready-made celeb fitting her description, not a half-baked one like Ziggy. Not that this is going to stop her spoiling the action for anyone else who is interested. Charley is a spoiler by nature. The real battle is between Emily and Chanelle, the two best-looking girls in the house and the two least independent. Both need their confidence reinforced by having a man in tow. Both spoilt. Charley is too confident for that. Carole is interested and 'flutters' girlishly around him. It is not a pretty sight. The rest look on slyly at the Roman circus.

The fight is sublimated into a battle over the hair straightening tongs. It is ferocious. Symbolically, Big Brother owns the tongs, which are battery operated and by all accounts rubbish. But their use for hours on end is vital to the girls functioning. Emily and Chanelle rip into each other verbally, repeatedly. The screaming reaches new heights. Emily uses a sort of rubbish logic. 'If you have these first then it will set a precedence of privilege which will be unacceptable in the house,' or something like it. Chanelle sprays tears around and has hissy fits. 'I can't help it if my hair has a curl.' On and on it goes.

This baffles Ziggy and, sitting at the table, he asks me about it. What do I know about such carryings on? I look at his little face. Just hours ago he was a tanned Adonis. Now there is fear and disbelief in his eyes. He has shrunk, too, and turned a strange yellow colour. How can I help him? He just wants a bit of what the girls shove in our faces. I briefly and sensitively break it to him that the tongs are his willy. Life is all about symbols. No wonder he looks haunted. Forty years ago, no twenty actually, I would have pushed them aside, got in there, had my way and it would all be over by now, Perhaps they have more time on their hands than I did.

The production team has asked what would cheer me up. I have told them I would like to leave for the night, go to Gravetye Manor, which is one of our favourite English hotels, and have dinner with David. If I could do this every day I would be quite happy to return to the fray, refreshed. Big Brother says it is all-powerful so I don't rule it out.

Meanwhile, by coincidence, they organise a dinner date in the black and white entrance hall. Each of us is to join Ziggy for one course of a meal. He is to be incarcerated within that room as he entertains us individually. Tracey and I are compatible in our preparations. Half an hour from start to finish including shower and hair and dressing is more than enough for both of us. We agree that we scrub up well. I like Tracey's outfit and secretly wish we were going out somewhere together, though not into a field. An odd thing happens. I have said something, I forget what, and Tracey laughs. She reaches forward and puts her hands on my shoulders and kisses me. While generally uncomfortable with the girls touchy feely business, this little gesture touches me out of all proportion. Coming from an unlikely source, it feels spontaneous and genuine, and my response alarms me. This is a dangerous world. A terribly lonely place.

How differently it might have turned out if I had gone and sat with Ziggy, eaten the half-decent plate of food, drunk the one glass of wine, and talked about tennis or golf.

Doctors say that smell is the most evocative of all the senses and the smell that I carry with me tonight is of peonies. In the corner of the room, which is the inner vestibule that marks the entrance to the house, there is a vase of a few rather straggly flowers. One is a peony. By chance I bought some cologne with me that I spray on the stiff sheets on the bed day and night to try to mask the smell of the bedroom. Julia, Winston's girl-friend, expresses her feelings about women quite succinctly, 'Always the stink of women! How I hate women!' The smell in the bedroom, that increases each day, is of sleep and dirty knickers, of towels used and dropped, the unmistakeable fishi-ness of women and of fetid disappointment.

On one level my cologne is a mistake. More than anything it reminds me of David and florists. I would put florists into Room 101. Had it been left to florists David and I would never have got together. We had only just met but David had decided that I should be his Final Wife. He knew that I was a stranger to kitchens and if we were ever to eat the responsibility would be his. He invited me to his house in Bath for supper. Just the two of us. I think of that night now. So much of this absurd arrangement in this corridor reminds me of that evening, if only by contrast. Then I took a gift. I thought about that this evening and nearly sacrificed some of my hidden stock of cashew nuts to present to Ziggy. Too precious, I decided.

It has been my experience that a useful tool in seducing a man is to give him flowers. It is surprising and flattering. Never take flowers as a gift to a hostess, by contrast, like Mrs Dalloway, she will have sorted that out much earlier and your gift will be a nuisance. The last thing she needs is to be looking for a vase with champagne getting warm and canapés getting cold.

In Bath I enlisted the help of a florist. A bunch, I asked, noth-ing formal, suitable for a man, a stylish man, an architect, perhaps all one colour, one type. Relinquishing control, a dangerous thing to do, I left her to it. So in a sense it was my fault when later that day I collected a strangled bridal thing of pink roses and gypsowhatever that I hate and pink ribbon that brings to mind My Little Pony and the twins, and is the very last thing likely to seduce anyone. I paid, took it home and threw it straight in the bin. But that is Bath for you. Never as chic as it thinks. I'm with Dickens, as ever, who called it a dreary little town. In a rage I dashed into my garden and cut the only thing in flower so that when I arrived at his house all David could see was an armful of blood red peonies and two little legs dangling beneath. So began an affair, but no thanks to florists.

I put this forward as my excuse for being in a sentimental, romantic frame of mind and for shoving the lad towards romance. I champion Chanelle's cause and damn Emily's. I am an accomplice in a train of events that is to spiral quickly into a sea of joyless recriminations. A bit like the nurse in Romeo and Juliet.

In Oceania heroism is empty because there is no one to save, but Ziggy is man enough to want to save Chanelle who, with her frightened eyes and slightly rounded shoulders and her pretending to be someone else, is ripe for the saving. It is odd later, looking back on events in the house at that time that I can never quite 'see' Ziggy. He is never quite in focus, never quite 'there'. Chanelle certainly needs saving from the anger of the other women as they sense her conquest. As she and Ziggy cuddle together in bed they must withstand the scorn of Laura, the raging frustration of Emily, the contempt of Charley and the knowledge that the whole sorry affair is being conducted day and night in front of anyone who chooses to turn on their television.

It seems to me to be an affair without passion or fire. I think again of Julia, a sexual being, who believes it doesn't matter what you say or do, that only feelings matter. I cannot tell, but I saw more passion in Ziggy's eyes when he showed me the photograph of Molly and in his stroking and fondling of Chanelle there is more dogginess than lust. Come on, you two, I want to shout. Get on with it. You might as well be hung for a sheep as a lamb, so to speak. In Oceania it is the aim of the authorities to abolish the orgasm. The group of baying girls has done it for them.

When we meet in the bathroom Ziggy asks my advice. I see no harm in him. He is a young man. He might be using her as part of his game, whether it is the game in the house or the general game of mating. He may want sex or a friend or both. Does it really matter? He is an attractive, sexy 26-year-old male. I thought these young people would be more adventurous and liberated. It would all have been done and dusted by now in my day. I advise him to proceed with caution. I catch the eye of the all-seeing camera, 'What would your mother think?' I personally think it is none of my business, but I am alone in that view.

Perhaps it is the smell of peony in the air or of unsatisfied sexual urges but the two come together in my thoughts as I have a chat with Gertrude. I have been missing Wilkie Collins. He would have had a view on all this. If there were a party or orgy or bacchanalia to be had, up would go the cry from Wilkie, 'I'm your man!' Wilkie exploded the Hollywood myth that you have to be good-looking to have a brilliant sex life. He was an ugly little man whose extraordinary personal life, indicating to me that he was good in bed. Look out here, handsome Ziggy. This brings to mind another smell.

Recently I read a copy of a science magazine. I wish I had it here with me now in this paperless house. There was news of an experiment, which had been conducted in Germany. It seems that no one has previously bothered to wonder at the tastes and preferences of sperm. What do they really like? An efficient German student decided to test which smells most interested the sperm. I laugh as I stroke Gertrude's dull leaves. She isn't thriving either. Imagine, Gertrude, an array of petri dishes full of the little chaps and tempting smells being wafted over them. Chanel No5, workman's armpits, bacon sandwiches... Nothing. Not a single response. Indifferent, even. It seemed that semen simply could not be bothered until, yes, and truly remarkably, lily of the valley. Immediately the little rascals were gambolling and giggling, or whatever semen does when over-excited and in party mood. There was no holding them back. None of this would have interested me too much except I had just been a recipient of a huge basket of toiletries. Soap, talcum powder, cologne, perfume, the works, in lily of the valley. I shudder to think the risks I have been taking. Looking back I swear I have heard the sound of thunder at three in the morning. I can see now it was the sound of the little buggers rushing down the M4 to get to me. Gertrude's branches shiver as a little breeze of frisson passes through them.

I am terribly hungry. Perhaps its all the sex. Not. Food here is a huge issue for me.

We have just had another task. We have been asked to stand by individual numbered podium. We are asked to rate ourselves in order of certain attributes from first to last. This is to be compared with Ziggy's evaluation and our shopping budget will be determined by how accurately we forecast his assessment. What follows is an undignified catfight and I am ashamed to be part of it.

Firstly, we must determine our comparative intelligence. I immediately step onto the podium marked 1. I judge that Ziggy will believe me to be the most intelligent. I am not saying that I am – by most standards I would be – but that Ziggy will say I am. Had I stabbed Emily in the eye with a knife it could not have caused more commotion. She is furious, mad like a rabid dog. I am calm. To shut her up I would move to number 307 but there is much at stake here and I cannot pander to her childishness. I do not give a toss about her assessment of my intelligence or me. At that moment my respect for these women is at its lowest and I care not a jot for their good opinion. What I do want, and think they should want, is the one hundred pounds that goes with getting the answer right. Being the only one listening to Big Brother's instructions, acting on them, and thereby winning one hundred pounds justifies me in thinking that I am the most intelligent, but that is by the way. Other evaluations follow like some primitive cattle market, most attractive, most co-operative.

There is further proof that we can never work as a team and there is no such thing as the sisterhood. But at least I have secured one hundred pounds for food for the group. If there is one defining moment from which Emily's fall began it is that moment when she takes the podium marked 2.

It is a relief that we shall have a better than basic food ration. The provisions that Big Brother initially supplied have dwindled alarmingly. No one else is concerned. But they aren't losing weight like I am. I can feel it falling from me. My own diet, as I have said, relies upon good ingredients simply cooked. It isn't difficult. But I am also trapped by my own body clock. I am up at 8 and in bed by one the next morning. I guess this, as we have no clocks. I am accustomed to regular meals. We all like to think that we are flexible, open to change, embracing variety. I have learnt that in matters of food I am a creature of routine. The girls eat crisps, and bread and toast and cereal all day. The main meal is being produced at 11 at night or sometimes later. If I were to follow this plan I would be ill, sooner, rather than later. It is not just the when it's the what. Supplies of fruit and salad are low and there are no juices or soft drinks. I am used to tap water but this is foul tasting.

Something else is going on. I realise what an emotive issue food is. Never is this more apparent than here. The kitchen and its use is the seat of power. Why? I am not used to a situation where who boils the carrots rules the roost. No one determines what I eat and when, especially when their decisions are clearly mad. Carole, Nicky and Laura rage continuously. In a way they are worse than the fights between the younger girls. They certainly impinge more on me. Typically, it is one o' clock. Lunchtime. I begin to prepare a salad for myself. No one else is up or if they are it is their breakfast time and they are making toast and cereal and creating havoc in the inadequate space. This doesn't matter. I just want to make a bowl of fresh ingredients with a little dressing. Carole or Laura or Nicky – most usually and increasingly Carole – stops me. Don't use that. Don't do that. Do it like that. Don't use balsamic vinegar, it's horrible. Don't put grapes in a salad; it's not right to mix fruit and salad. You know the girls don't like cheese, they say it smells. The list, the intrusion, the bullying is endless.

One day Carole standing at my shoulder, shedding hair on the work surface, is too much for me and I leave and walk in to the bedroom. I put my head under the duvet and kneeling on the floor sob into my bed. Emily comes past and stops and says 'are you all right...what are you doing?' 'I am all right,' I reply. 'I am just sniffing my mattress'.

Sometimes I achieve some food and take it to the table. I make a civilised place for myself with bowl and plate and cutlery and plastic mug and a little napkin folded from a piece of paper napkin that I am eking out. I respect myself and this is reflected in the small ways I treat Me. I struggle against the tide of their tyranny but I know I am drowning. And its all so unnecessary.

I know how it looks. It is seen as me setting myself apart. I can view it from the other side of the camera. A lonely old lady choosing to distance herself in her own aura of snobbishness. No, I just need to eat and to eat with dignity. When we do eat together it is a miserable business. I look across at the cooking area at the mounds of ingredients being boiled and fried. It is a case of the three witches, stirring and hatching plots against each other.

Nicky has standards and I would eat her food any day but with Carole in particular I see the spectre of illness. Meat is taken from the fridge, left to defrost in the sun, put back in the fridge, sun, fridge. Everything is frozen. Everything goes in to the freezer. The milk is always solid. I ask why. I am too marginalized to be heard. 'Why is the milk always frozen?' I chip a little out of the carton to put in the tea. I hear Tracey saying that all I want is Gordon Ramsey. 'Gordon Fucking Ramsey,' she says. I just want to be left to gather a few bits for myself. It doesn't take me a minute. I eat virtually nothing but I can see Emily eyeing up what I have on my plate. 'How much cheese have you got there?' she asks.

They say they love food. They know nothing about it. I just hope their sex lives are better than their food. Food to me is about taste and smell and sight and atmosphere. But above all, it is about love. I can't queue in line at eleven at night holding out my plate for some grey mass of tasteless splodge that I have seen prepared in the most unsanitary way. It is handed out with spite and martyrdom in equal measures. I don't eat plated food. I don't eat amid an atmosphere of anger. I hate myself for loathing the way they eat, their silly eating fads, and the rubbish they crave. I long for a simple cheese sandwich made for me with love. I see Ziggy go hungry because he is a man and needs more. I have a salad on my plate. Fingers reach out and pick from the little cheese I have grated in to a bowl. Laura says, 'Big people need more food.' She isn't joking. Carole's nightie and Laura's dressing gown are impregnated with food. Nose wiping. Bottom scratching. Picking.

Charley is standing by the table. Her minute shorts are level with the top of the table. I lift my knife and fork to eat the salad. Charley digs her nails deep in to her crotch. Her thrush, she tells us, always ever-present, is worse today. Carole, her plate overflowing with boiled vegetables, elbows on table, chin glistening, gives her detailed advice. Scratch. Scratch. I push away my plate.

I hear it said that Lesley goes missing. I think they mean physically, though how that is possible in this confinement I don't know, but I try. I am certainly missing mentally most of the time.

I take my surface wipes to the lavatory. I wipe the door, the basin and the lavatory seat. I take a book to read from the library in my head. I am most confident when reading Dickens, remembering whole chunks. As time passes I am finding this too painful. Too many memories. I am safer with good old Wilkie and I am half way through The Woman in White. There are no locks on the doors and the cameras watch me.

Sometimes I speak out loud. I am on Mastermind. I am successfully through to the second round. My first round specialist subject was the private life of Charles Dickens. My second round is Tescos Antiseptic Wipes. I have swotted from the back of the packet. I am an expert. The questioning is tough. 'What is the telephone number of the Tescos Antiseptic Wipe help-line?'

I am avoiding the Diary Room, and Big Brother is leaving me alone. The two-day deadline will pass unmarked. Once I go into to room and talk to the camera on the wall. I don't want a dialogue. I just want to expunge those ugly screaming voices with their foul language and bleak thoughts from my head.

They ask if I were to write a book of my life, how much would my Big Brother experience figure? Not meaning to be hurtful, since I judge it is difficult to be cruel to a wall, though David, as an architect might disagree, I say it would take up half a page. I can sense disappointment. I cover up quickly by saying, with a bit of padding out, it might make a chapter.

Prompted by something the hidden girl says, I speak about our Croatian trip.

I think that David and I are robust. At least until this Big Brother experience I always thought so. There is plenty of evidence for and our experience in Croatia supports this. Not everyone would have chosen to drive through the country in 1995 at the height of the war there, in order to spend six months on a tiny island far out into the Adriatic. Many would have turned back early in the journey. Only the very intrepid would have carried on after having seen off the last of the Volvos in the trendy areas of Italy. But, no, we carried on down the Croatian coast admiring the fabulous seascape, commenting on the empty roads and the presence of U.N. vehicles and troop carriers.

Accommodation was difficult to find. All the large tourist hotels have been commandeered for refugees fleeing for their lives and only those willing to exploit two elderly British going in the other direction were willing to take us in. We paid Ritz prices to stay in bed and no breakfast rooms that left us flea-ridden and exhausted. We pressed on with the thought that at the end would be an idyllic holiday home rented to us by a man David met at a party. 'What are you doing for the summer?' he had asked. David answered vaguely, 'Probably get away from it all.' 'Then have my mother in laws house in Croatia for six months,' he said, omitting to mention the war raging there. In fairness I have to say that we wouldn't have been deterred as I have always said that the best time to visit a country is just after a war. Going in the middle of one might seem a logical extension of this.

After a couple of days of coastal struggle and wearying of the sea view I suggested brightly, 'what about a picnic?' We gathered a few meagre supplies from a struggling market and, consulting the map, set off inland. Until now the signs of actual battle had been confined to the effect on the civilian population. We had seen evidence of ethnic cleansing. A chilling phrase. Driving through small towns, ordinary places that could be seen the world over, through suburban streets, we saw missing houses. Rows of houses with just one destroyed like a blackened tooth. A child's bicycle on its side, a pet dog lying miserable and abandoned left to fend for itself. Not knowing quite what we are seeing. Was that where the people lived who we had seen crowded six families to a room in the tourist hotels? Or were they picking up the rotten carrots under the wooden tables in the market? Was that their Granny being pushed aside by a younger woman for the prize of a few cabbage leaves in the gutter? We didn't understand, but were frightened by what we imagined. Some English speaking students told us to keep hidden our Serbo/Croat into English dictionary which they told us could threaten our lives with its implication that the Serbs and the Croats shared even a common language.

One man told me that he was glad to see his neighbour go. He told me he was a good worker, a good family man and the two families had got on well, but they were Serbs and had to go. He shrugged. 'They were Serbs. They came to my country and took over the schools, the hospitals, the jobs and houses. They had to go.' He talked about the eleventh century and I was lost in the jumble of ancient ethnic history.

Inland we still saw the derelict houses amid untended farmland but the air seemed fresher and our mood lifted. Suddenly, however, the air began to thicken and become overcast. Just our luck for the weather to change. 'I think we are in for rain,' I say. I blinked several times. It is as though we have entered a light fog. 'Any worse and we shall have to put on our headlights.' It is mid-day. With hindsight we should have had more sense. There are tanks on either side of us. Burning tanks. Smoke floating from them, drifting across the fields into our path. The silence, too, should have warned us. Not just the eerie silence around us but the absolute emptiness inside the car. Just David's white knuckles as he gripped the steering wheel and me holding our British passports like some ancient talisman.

There is no one in sight until from behind a hedge five men move out to stand by the side of the road. My experience of soldiers is confined to Horse Guards parade and marching bands. For me dirt and death don't come in to it. These men, standing so silently by the roadside, watching us, are terrifying. They carried not just one but dozens of guns strung around their shoulders, across their chests, round their waists and in their hands. They wore no uniforms but dark clothes, scruffy and ragged. It was their beards that most impressed me. Great thick black beards like some terrible children's storybook, pantomime beards fastened behind the ear with wires. Wordlessly, barely breathing, eyes fixed ahead, David drove on. We could see the mountains ahead. I spoke. 'It sounds like thunder. Perhaps it will rain.' Rain on our picnic being the least of our problems.

The suddenly we weren't so safe in our Volvo cocoon. Men were moving out of nowhere, surrounding us. We stop. A bazooka is pushed through my open window and rests in my lap. A gun is pressed to David's temple. These were a different lot. No beards, instead a sense of urgency. More volatile. More dangerous. One spoke English and this we agreed later saved our lives. 'What are you doing here?' Holding our passports gave me strength. I talk to him. I hear my voice as though from a distance. All British Raj and Empire. I pointed to the map under the bazooka. 'We are going for a picnic in the mountains.' There was silence. The seconds tick by slowly as we listen to the thunder of guns and the whistle of snipers and smell the burning in the air. He spoke to the others. Silence, while they think of their options. Then laughter. They laughed, throwing back their heads like men who haven't laughed for years. Finally he said, 'You are thirty yards from the front line.' He pointed ahead to an abandoned U.N. sentry box. 'Turn back quick.'

We have thought since of contacting Volvo with a view to telling them about the three point turn that David executed at high speed, and of the way the Volvo held a straight line while driver and passenger closed their eyes and drove past the bearded Serbian warriors for the second time.

I tell the girl, masquerading as Big Brother, that later that day I complained about the tepid water in a hotel that had been shelled the previous day. 'You complained about the water?' For once Big Brother is incredulous. 'You complained about the water in a war torn country?' 'Standards,' I say. Standards.

Silence for a long time. Finally broken by Big Brother. 'Are you insane, Lesley?' I consider this. 'Yes.'

Big Brother asks me what, without trivialising the situation in a war torn country, what is the difference for me of that experience and this, the Big Brother house. This brings me up short. I don't yet want to be back in this experience. There is one big difference that makes that tolerable and this intolerable. I answer truthfully. 'David.'

I leave the Diary Room.

Back in the sitting room I take a banana, my last, from its hiding place. I place it on a plate with cutlery and half a paper napkin. I wash my hands. Seated, I cut the banana and eat it with the knife and fork, wiping my mouth between bites. Welcome to my world.

Chapter Eleven

Big Brother has closed the bathroom as a punishment for some minor infringement of the rules. I suspect this has been manufactured by Big Brother. I am sure that when the cunning designers thought up the plan to have the bath in the sitting room they had not reckoned that our resident washerwoman would turn it into a little piece of Victorian East End slum. This closing of the bathroom and loss of shower might well be an attempt to create some racy photo opportunities. This, after all, is a television game show. They are in for a disappointment.

I am the first to venture to bathe in front of millions of people. First I have to scrub the bath. It is a major job removing the hairs and filth caused by the clothes 'washing'. I guess I spend forty minutes on that. Then I fill the bath using a whole bottle of foam bath so that the bath is only half full but the foam laps over the edge. I get in to the bath wearing bra and pants and draped with a thin dressing gown. It will not make the front cover of Nuts. For someone who is normally never more than a couple of hours away from a bath and does not even share a bathroom with her husband, I am finding the arrangements here relatively satisfactory. I do resent the closure of the bathroom, as I am the only person who stands to suffer as a result, but I have managed to move all my morning activities to the sitting room quite successfully. Ziggy moves with me. The lavatory is more problematic. What with Wilkie Collins, the Mastermind crew, occasionally John Ruskin, the Big Brother production team and the possibility of four million people, it is a crowded space. As a result I am constipated.

My plans for leaving have been put on hold. All was going so well.

Big Brother gave Ziggy the job of nominating two people for Friday's evictions one of whom would go home as a result of public voting. Please may it me, Ziggy.

He has chosen Emily and Shabs, on the basis that they have contributed least to the house. Damn, I knew I shouldn't let him see me clean the bath. Emily has tricked Ziggy in to revealing that he nominated her and he is furious. I have seen him angry and upset before. Not long after he came in to the house, the girls formed a pack and chased him around the garden and into the house. Cornering him in the sitting room they pulled at his shorts. It was an ugly scene that resulted in him having a bloody foot and I considered he was lucky, given the ferocity of the attack, to have come off so lightly. How do these things look to the outside world? It wasn't funny or entertaining and made me wonder what the reaction would have been if Ziggy had been a girl and it had been a wild pack of blokes.

Shabs has taken the news of her possible eviction philosophically. She appears to have accepted that being evicted is preferable to the dreaded 'walking'. Well done me. She is now likely to leave on Friday and is busy contemplating her 'deals'. When she isn't fighting or scratching, Charley is crying. She says she worries that people outside won't like her. She doesn't give a thought for Shabs, her declared Best Friend. 'I don't think they are going to like me,' she wails, constantly. 'Some will like you. Some will not. It is the same for all of us,' I tell her. I could add that she might think about it before she tears in to her next victim. But I don't.

Emily has taken charge of our first shopping list. I ask for fruit and salad, and Shabs wants chocolate. Otherwise I leave her to it. It is strange that those who do the cooking do not want to be involved in the shopping list. Ziggy is right about Emily. She does contribute nothing to the house, except a good figure and a skimpy bikini, which I do not underestimate, and she is the least suitable person to do the shopping. That is proved when the provisions are delivered. It consists almost exclusively of packets of crisp and cigarettes. Emily's idea of fruit is one expensive pineapple. People are surprisingly relaxed about this, though Charley is scathing about the pineapple. Seeing good-natured Shabs' face fall at the absence of chocolate I retrieve my stashed bar and share it with her.

I have decided to go easy on Emily in future. I had a Road to Damascus moment in the middle of the night. I couldn't have been asleep for very long when I woke with a start. An unusual feeling engulfed me. A feeling of guilt. I felt that I had been doing the wrong thing in engaging in sniping with Emily, however mutual. Haunted in the night by that sad blue dress, I can see that beneath the bravado she really is quite a little girl. I have no experience of these girls. My daughter and I were so very different from them. In the morning I try to make moves towards her and we have a neat enough little chat about her ambitions and talents.

Too little, too late. That night I wake again. This time it is to hear the voice of Big Brother telling Emily to go to the Diary Room. I am sensitive to the different voices and the differing tones. Not only is it the middle of the night but, rarely, everyone is asleep. No one moves. I sit up and in the light as she opens the bedroom door I see her leave. She is wearing a yellow dress. Instinct tells me that we shall not see her again.

The details will emerge later but it does not surprise me. I cannot say that I could have predicted the precise nature of her downfall, but from the first moment she walked in I felt that her presence in the house was doomed.

In the morning people are slow to realise that she has gone. Big Brother calls me to the Diary Room and gives me a notice to read out. It tells that Emily has been removed because she has broken a fundamental rule of the house. It is heavy stuff. I hear my voice as I read. I over-egg but I want the girls to listen because the notice carries with it a serious warning to us all. People **are** watching you. Not one single action or word goes unnoticed. We are so vulnerable. I don't know Trotsky's attitude to meetings but even Carole sits for this one.

The production team has asked me to pack Emily's case. We collect it from the storeroom. I decide to delegate her packing to the twins. They have been friends with Emily and are confused and distressed. They will be good at this job and it will give them something to focus on while they come to terms with what has happened. A bit like a funeral. Part of my motivation is that I wouldn't know Emily's things from anyone else's'. It is all such a mess but the twins should be able to disentangle the chaos. Laura makes me angry as she insists they aren't capable but interference is what one has come to expect from the trio of 'mothers'.

Meanwhile, for once, Shabs and Charley are quiet. Charley is chewing on her knuckles and looking especially thoughtful. She looks like she is weighing up the implications to herself of recent events. She and Nicky talk quietly together about what prompted the departure. The air is thick with self-righteous indignation. I know what has happened. I don't know the details and it is not until some days later that I ask Laura, in a quiet moment, for the precise nature of the conversation that had taken place. Even then, since I wasn't there, I cannot be sure. I am glad that so often, despite knowing that it risks making me appear aloof, I move away from scenes of confrontation and conflict, not wishing even by my physical presence to be seen to be complicit in it. It is a stress but worth it.

It is the very thing that I have feared right from the early audition. It would be a hard heart indeed that, knowing the pressures of living in that terrible environment, did not feel for Emily.

A day or so after we arrived in the house we were confined to the bedroom and the interconnecting doors were locked. When we were released we found that photographs had appeared around the bath area. These are Polaroid snaps taken at early audition and are virtually unrecognisable. They are backlit. There are empty spaces, presumably for new housemates. I contemplate what will happen to Emily's photograph now she has gone. Will it be removed or will the light behind it simply be turned off? In 'Nineteen Eighty Four' every trace of Emily would be removed from the records and from our memories, and, with time, it would be as though she had never existed.

I have spoken to the twins about Emily. They have taken her going badly and they remind me so much of our kittens when they first arrived in our house, abandoned and dumped over the wall. Like them the twins huddle together on the bed. I can hardly bear it. I, too, am afraid. This is what haunts me day and night in this place. This saying or doing the wrong thing so dreadfully publicly and not a chance to turn back the clock. As I speak to the twins I know my tone is unbearably patronising, but I speak as much to myself as to them, 'Emily will be all right. She has a mummy and a daddy and they will look after her.' I hope I am right.

We all gather in the sitting room. It is quiet and stilted. It is impossible to know what they are thinking and they never communicate at the best of times. I tell them, 'It is a form of bereavement.' Chanelle complains that the nails on her right hand are not growing as fast as the nails on her left hand. She is entirely selfish. But perhaps bereavement affects us all differently.

Carole is busy collecting up the mugs. Charley, whether by design or habit I cannot say, is singing an annoying song that Emily introduced into the house and which the girls have been singing repetitively ever since. Something about asking for a Mercedes Benz. I consider who I shall hit. Carole or Charley. I have been talking about my membership of the W.I. I can see the headlines now. W.I. member strangles London not-it girl. Gloucestershire luminary shoves bearded lady's head through mangle. I remember the rule about physical violence and risk the Thought Police by dwelling deliciously on the two thoughts.

I also have the secret of my going to consider. Because I care for them, though I don't think they are the silly babies that others do, I think it only fair to pre-warn the twins. I have a chat with them. I ask that if I were to leave – stressing that I would not go in the way that Emily did – that they would pack my case for me. I tell them that it would be very easy because, as they can see, each day my things are neatly arranged in small piles on my bed. I would leave another smaller pile on the floor which would be things they should distribute among the housemates as they see fit. I stress that only they should do my packing.

Though goodness knows when I can go now. The eviction has been cancelled. You can't have an eviction with only one evictee. Shabs has been reprieved, much to her disappointment, and I need to bide my time. For some reason I am mindful of the producers' needs if I can guess what they might be.

I see what Carole is doing with the mugs that she has gathered together, she has a nasty cold sore on her lip that has erupted in the last few days. Call me Miss Picky, but I don't want to catch it. I am struggling to keep body and soul together as it is. My exercise plan has had to be modified but each morning when I get up I can achieve a few basics. I also walk quickly around and across the courtyard like a prisoner, which I am. But in all respects I am feeling vulnerable and can do without herpes on top of everything else. Basic hygiene is good sense. I paint a dot of nail varnish on the bottom of a mug and tell the housemates that this is mine. I try to make as little of this as possible but I accept that it will not go down well. They should see my ritual cleaning of the lavatory. Now, that really would upset them.

Carole has amused herself, and the others, by painting similar marks on the base of all the mugs. She has, however, made the fatal mistake of engaging Charley as her accomplice. Charley is sent to keep me in conversation in the bedroom. Nothing could have alerted me better than this. What larks, Carole. It is steadily becoming Carole's house, rather than Big Brother's, and I wonder when they will take action to retrieve it from her. She tells the others what she is doing and they wait to see my reaction. There is none. I have already secreted 'my' mug under my bed and use it and then put it back. In any case, Carole, I am leaving.

Relationships ebb and flow in the house. At the moment I can see that Charley and Carole are becoming unlikely kindred spirits. I know that amateur psychologists would say that we reject in others what we most dislike in ourselves. I can see nothing of myself in them.

Carole has been interviewing us all for some radio show in connection with Big Brother. She holds a microphone in front of me and asks about my experience of being in the house. I say that, for the benefit of older listeners, life in Big Brother house most closely equates to an old television series called Tenko, but without the laughs.

The girls and Ziggy have set up an obstacle course in the garden. They time themselves against their own counting. I watch their lovely, clean, fresh bodies as they dash about. Tracey and I have a go, to be sociable, but soon retire to the smoker's bench. Tracey says, 'I liked that so much I'm not going to do it again.' I wish I had said that. It is a strange social experiment that sees us thrown together.

As we sit in companionable silence like two old ladies watching children at the park, I remember my days in Cambridge. I have discovered that I lived close to Tracey's mother. Tracey tells me that she doesn't own a passport. She has never been on a plane. From these snippets, rare as gold dust, I am building up a picture. Some of the least interesting people I have met have travelled the most. For some reason I think of a man I knew who lived at Cromer, a wholly incomprehensible choice for a free man to make. He was a Reuter's correspondent. He had been everywhere in the world. He had met everyone worth meeting since Jesus including Elvis, Ghandi, Einstein, Marilyn Monroe and Baden Powell, though not at the same time, in the same room, which was a pity in itself. He claimed that Lawrence of Arabia had made a pass at him and, more remarkably perhaps, Lawrence Olivier had not. He had been at all the major summit meetings during the middle of the twentieth century, when the world was carved up in to the mess it is now, and he had witnessed atom bombs being dropped.

The truly remarkable thing about this man was that none of this had made him the least bit interesting and he wins my Most Boring Man I Have Ever Met Award – an honour for which there has been enormous competition over the years.

Emily's photograph remains lit and Charley hums the annoying song that Emily taught her. She isn't spoken of again.

CHAPTER TWELVE

I have been in the house for nine days and it feels like a life sentence. I pluck at straws to entertain myself. I have never once been bored in my life, have never used the word or allowed it to be used. Only people who can't read are bored. Only people without inner resources are bored. Only people with no social skills are bored.

There are highlights in the day. Carole is an unemployed sexual health worker. She asks us if we know how many sperm there are in teaspoon of semen. She has told me about a course she helped with, when young people were given a doll to look after and taken to a holiday camp to show them the downside of parenting. I should think the holiday camp bit might be warning enough. I don't know if spoons and sperm were involved there. I can only marvel at the paucity of my sex life that I have never seen sperm in a teaspoon.

That I contemplate this long after a sane person would have moved on, is testament to my boredom. Chanelle is confident, 'Ten million.' I am now borderline clinically depressed and plump for, 'Three.' Still less do I care. I consider telling them about the German experiment and the lily of the valley. Events overtake us. Carole has finished sewing back Betsy's head. Betsy is Chanelle's stuffed rabbit and Chanelle is nineteen. Jumping up, Chanelle takes Betsy, who is the only person in the house who I truly hate, and rushes off to the bedroom. 'I must show Betsy to Ziggy'. Lucky Ziggy. Ziggy is twenty-six.

The inevitability of breaking down is becoming overwhelming.

Hang on. We have our third task in nine days. We have break danced and fought over the podium game. This time we are to sculpt models of each other in clay. I love the apron I am given to wear. Perhaps it is the small things that engage one in such a dull environment or the novelty of it. I have never worn an apron in my life or had the need to. I would also, in the outside world, have to be careful, being married to an architect, for fear that people would think that I was trying to emulate Ruthie Rogers and wanted to open a café.

No one watching these pathetic tasks can fully appreciate how we housemates fall on them with excitement. It is only through driving us to utter boredom that Big Brother can get us to so happily embrace their playgroup activities and risk their humiliation. This proves to be quite a jolly task. Within five minutes I have a fair likeness of Shabs in clay in front of me. Or is it Medusa? Shabs is modelling me. Unfortunately I finish my uncanny likeness at the very moment that Big Brother announces that we only have one more hour to complete our creations. 'The true artist knows when they have achieved perfection,' I announce.

Everything here takes forever and drains activities of fun and spontaneity. Hours later we are to present our completed work, one by one, to the camera and describe our inspirations. Charley wants more time. She is obsessive in her detailing and is really engrossed in it. Some are pathetic, some are brilliant. When I present mine I predict that at this very minute a cheque is winging its way from Charles Saatchi to buy it. Blank faces. Shabs, when presenting mine, says, 'It's the thought that counts.' She is such a strange and lovely girl. She has made animals as well as my head, a veritable zoo and talks about Lesley's journey into the Big Brother house as though through a jungle. So, she's not so daft really. Chanelle makes huge breasts for her model of Laura. We all chip in with extra clay.

The task is over and we are sitting about, talking. Chanelle is telling us about how long the Beckhams have been married. The twins tell me that they have to do their chores. Why are they telling me? It seems that Carole has told them that they can't go out until they have done the 'chores'.

I tell them to get out in the sun instead. I hate seeing these young people dragged into drudgery. Nicky asks me about finding a man. Chanelle is applying makeup. She is only truly content when not distracted from herself. As the days have passed she looks less and less like Victoria. I think she may be killing the goose that lays the golden egg but once the media moguls take her over it will be back to her third rate performance. I sit very close to her and watch, like a child might watch its mother. It is a complicated business and one I am well out of.

I keep thinking of Muffin the Mule and Andy Pandy. I feel that the inside of my brain is breaking down like the reception on a mobile telephone. I have to fight harder and harder to remember what once a couple of weeks ago would come unbidden. I have finished Woman in White and am back to Dickens and I am struggling through some Christmas stories.

I have made a salad for everyone. I can hear Nicky complaining that I have used too much cheese. The twins say that they don't like cheese, as it smells 'off'. I take a spoon and while they watch I remove the cheese and put it in a bowl.

In the bedroom I take out all my clothes from the drawers under the bed. I shake them individually and lay them out. They are fresh and clean. I have thrown away, down the shoot in the kitchen, a La Perla underwear set and a white shirt that I have been bathing in. I change in to a little black frock. It is a Diane von Furstenberg – not a wrap around which makes me look like a fifties cleaning lady – but a button down the front job. It looks business-like, neat and serious. I go through to the sitting room and press the button at the Diary Room. A camera swivels to have a closer look at me. I am going through to see Big Brother.

It was agreed on Sunday that we would talk again after I have had a chance to think over my request to leave. It is now Friday. I have stayed to see people through Emily's leaving and in case of Friday evictions. Fresh people, I guess, will be coming in tonight.

I tell the camera in the diary room that I wish to leave in the morning. It is a long conversation. While the production team makes an attempt to get me to stay, I do not feel their hearts are truly in it. It is necessary, however, to play out the scene for the purpose of the taped recording. I try to be as fair as possible towards the other housemates. I say, 'They are lovely people and they are infuriating people.' When pressed I will not budge from saying that they have been truly gracious to me.

Like everything, I believe this to be neither true nor a lie. Sometimes I have been bullied, other times I have felt valued, sometimes loved, sometimes hated, scorned, despised, revered. The truth is not a straightforward matter. I am not prepared to put my unhappiness in the laps of the housemates. It is, after all, a game and they are playing it better than I am. I have said to Nicky, in the context of her ever lasting anguish about food and men, 'you must not make the mistake of feeling responsible for other people's happiness. You can only do your best. If they are unhappy that is their responsibility, not yours.'

They, the production team, ask for reasons for my leaving. I cite hygiene, lack of sleep and the issue of meals. That is sufficient. I am weary. There would be no way I could last this out for a further eleven weeks and I cannot count on being voted out quickly. I think of an earlier statement I made that the public would either love me or hate me, and that in either case might just keep me in.

In that moment looking back over the last days I cannot think that anyone could like me. Even those with great insight would not be able to see past my crying, and selfishness and isolation and glib remarks, to the very great effort that I have been making with housemates.

The disembodied voice asks how I feel about me taking away the democratic right of the public to vote and determine the outcome of the competition. I want to laugh at this absolute pomposity. It is a game show where we dress up in silly costumes and compete in humiliating games, in uncongenial company, under the stress of a hostile environment, to win basic foodstuffs. The ultimate prize, according to the girls, is to sit in the V.I.P enclosure at some half-baked club in London and take your clothes off for Nuts. Please do not bring David and the Normandy landings and all the very real fights for freedom and democracy in to this.

In any case I know that if I 'walk' it will be better to do it sooner, before anyone can level the accusation of wasting his or her telephone money on voting for me. They can get someone in quick to refute the bogus claim that I have taken a place from another hapless person. I feel sure that, as we speak, someone is locked in that little cell in Elstree studio being frisked to take my place.

It is a long interview but we both know the outcome. Finally, to be sure, I play my trump card. If they do not let me out through a door I shall scale the walls and they will run the risk of newspaper headlines, 'W.I. member caught on barbed wire escaping from Big Brother house.' There is a slight laugh and an agreement that I should come to the Diary Room in the morning to leave. I am Captain Oates after all.

In the sitting room everyone is preparing for this evening's live show. They are convinced that more men will be arriving. I go out to the garden and sit by Gertrude and indulge in thinking of my secret, forbidden yearnings. In my head I can already smell real coffee.

All week there has been the occasional helicopter overhead. It is said that newspapers hire them to take photographs of housemates and I have joked that it is the chance of seeing Carole in her swimsuit that draws them. The others say it is David coming to get me. There is one overhead now and the speakers tell us to get indoors and the shutters come down. Don't lower the rope now, David. It is too late.

That evening we gather at the sofas, primped and preened to await the arrival of the men. It is unlikely that anyone of us will leave, but the tension, unimaginable to anyone who hasn't experienced it, is electric. The sound of crowds calling and screaming is played for hours on an everlasting loop. It is maddening and designed not just to cover the sound of the real thing outside, but also to add to our considerable personal and group tension. There is a primitive clinging together and a feeling of being a cohesive community that is missing in the rest of the week.

Finally the newcomer arrives, bursting through the door, a giant of a man, dark and unmistakeably Greek, vibrant and glamorous, his clothes a tribute to bondage. He kisses my hand and says, 'A classy lady.' He is intelligent. I look across at Ziggy's face. It is a study in conflict. Is he relieved or disappointed? Gerry is as camp as they come. Clever, Big Brother.

Then, just when we think it can't get worse, the doors open again and Laura, who likes the first word, says, 'A clown.' He is a funny little Irish chap wearing jolly clothes, as she says, like a clown. Neither gay nor straight, in my opinion, but time will tell. The disappointment is palpable. It is almost too much for Charley to bear. I want to laugh.

The newcomers are made much of by the girls. The Irish chap, Seany, a sort of poor mans Mick Hucknell but not so handsome, hisses quietly at me so I hardly hear what he says. 'Hello, four eyes.' I may be mistaken. I am shocked, not by the rudeness, but by the antiquity of the insult. I thought that had gone out of usage years ago. Perhaps not in Liverpool from whence Seany hails. Good. I have had some of the best times of my life in Ireland. He is a curious cove and is already complaining about the state of the house, remonstrating about the filth of the sofas, the dirt in the bath, so perhaps we aren't entirely without common ground.

Later, there is talk about the sleeping arrangements. Ziggy is agitated. He does not wish to share a bed with another man. I can understand this. While I don't want anyone to know I am going in the morning I tell him that tomorrow it will be resolved and he should just get through tonight.

There is much excitement in the air. I go to bed at around 1.00 as usual, I guess, and leave the others to play. Seany has been auditioning for Big Brother since it was launched eight

years ago and he is overwrought. The girls, as ever, love to
party which means screaming, and shouting, and jumping. It is
good to hear this in a positive way for a change.

At 4.00 in the morning, I think, I am as deeply asleep as I can
get in that place. I hear whispering which is unusual, no one is
usually that sensitive and the next thing my duvet is whipped
away from me. So cruel. No one can know that my great fear
in life centres around my poor eyesight. For the last years of her
life my mother was blind and, while I have no reason to expect
that to happen to me, it will have left me with some residual
anxiety. So, in the night, in the dark, it is not my dignity that
first concerns me but my spectacles. I hunt around for them. I
am afraid in my confusion, or in the stampeding hysteria of the
herd, they may be lost or broken.

I am afraid, too, that further, worse attacks will take place.
I find my spectacles, put them on and sit on the bed. It is Seany,
obviously encouraged by Shabs and Charley, who has done the
deed. Later, it is said that this 'duvet-gate' as it in known in Big
Brother circles, was the deciding factor in my leaving. The decision had been made and it was done and dusted. In any case
had it not been I am uncertain that Seany's hysteria and instability would have driven me out. Had there been no support
from Big Brother that would have make me reach for my case
but we are not to know. But what is certain is that it was
Laura's words that would have made up my mind. 'You
shouldn't do that to an old woman.'

You shouldn't do that to an old woman. I wonder what
would have happened if the victim had been Laura and I had
said, 'You should not do that to a fat woman.'

The only civilised response is to walk away.

Prank. I hear the word 'prank'. As I lay in bed during what
was left of my final night the word took me back to Portugal
again. To a quiet and innocent village called Sao Bartolomeu de
Messines where dozens of its women were a victim of a cruel
hoax some years back. The tranquillity of the place was
severely disrupted when several respectable Portuguese ladies

stripped to the waist, went into the streets and pointed their breasts at the sky. All this was reported in the local paper.

They had received a telephone call purporting to come from the Faro Laboratory – a medical centre – saying that a great leap in medical science meant that they could now have a mammography examination done by satellite through a laser beam. Reasonably enough, women jumped at this opportunity and spent some minutes stripped to the waist on their balconies or out on the street. Some were told that they would experience side effects in the form of sexual pleasure and were promised an unforgettable afternoon.

One lady reported she was in telephonic contact with the 'doctor' during the procedure which in her case took place on the top of a wall along the main road. Complaints were made to the police but I do not know the outcome.

That, Seany, is one hell of a prank.

CHAPTER THIRTEEN

In the morning when, at last, everyone is asleep, I get up and go through my ritual of taking out my clothes and laying them out on the bed. I could do this in my sleep and in the dark.

The bathroom is open for us to use again. I wash my hair, shower and do my makeup. I go through to the sitting room and throw my wet clothes down the rubbish shoot. I don't want wet clothes in my suitcase. There are pencil drawings on the doors. Bottles in this. Cardboard in that. No mention of wet underwear.

I make tea. The door to the garden is not unlocked yet. Looking out I see that it is a fresh clear day. I didn't want to go home in the rain.

It is not Ziggy, but Gerry, the Greek intellectual, who joins me and we sit on the sofa and talk. Well, Gerry talks. We have interests in common and I can see that it would have been a welcome relief to have someone to talk to. Except he does all the talking and I know that even he would soon become tedious in such a confined space. I also see that some of the light and excitement has gone from his eyes. He is too clever not to be already disappointed. I guess we have more in common than art and literature. I ask his birth date and it is the same day and month as mine. Though not the same year. He tells me about his family and that I remind him of his grandmother. He has problems within his family because of his being gay which surprises me, as I thought the Greeks invented it. He tells me that he has come in to the house so that when he gets out more people will want to sleep with him. 'Boys' he calls them, as he likes younger men, 20 or 22. I think of Chanelle and Ziggy who

get so much aggro from the other because of their age difference. When you have a 22-year age gap between yourself and
your husband, as I do, seven years is nothing.

Perhaps it is the birth sign, but we share a penchant for
strawberry blondes. On that basis I fancy Cate Blanchett but
whether Andrew Marr can be described as strawberry blonde
is pushing it a bit.

Gerry is not a person who requires a contributing audience
so it is quite pleasant just to sit there sipping tea and half-
listening. I feel sad for him. He is looking for acceptance and
affirmation. He really is going to find it hard in here. After an
hour or so I think it time to get ready. I don't want him bonding with me. There aren't going to be too many people who are
going to listen so well.

I get dressed. It is traditional to bring in an eviction night
outfit, which is saved for that night. Mine is brighter and live-
lier than the black and white outfits that I have been wearing. I
judge it best not to look too cheerful in this ignominious exit so
choose instead another, as yet unworn, white jacket. I don't
know what to expect when I leave.

No one stirs in the bedroom so I re-arrange my things on the
bed for the last time. I place my toilet roll and the last of the
cashew nuts by Tracey's bed and leave a pile of toiletries by the
cooker. When I am sure that everything is as straightforward as
possible for the twins and their pre-arranged packing, I go to
the Diary Room.

There, Big Brother asks me to go through all my reasons for
leaving. It is the same monologue as yesterday. I guess that, as
always, it is for the benefit of the whirring cameras and tapes
and their multifarious uses. I am careful, again and as ever, in
what I say. I am anxious not to have a hint of a falling out with
the production team. I have never been able to judge how they
feel about me. It would be impossible to do so. I think there
are more than 500 people in the team and over the months I
have met or seen so many of them. They give nothing away.
While I have not always liked what they have done, they have

always been absolutely charming to me. I know that they are part of a huge – some would say ruthless – larger machine, but I shall judge things on a personal level. I can have no complaint. There are changes and suggestions I would wish to make but I admire their single-mindedness and attention to detail, much like my own.

I wasn't coerced, bribed or threatened. No one lied to me. I was free to leave or walk at any minute. I could have no serious complaint. I had read 'Nineteen Eighty Four'. It was a game I volunteered for. It just wasn't a game that was important enough for me to suffer to win. No one will die because I leave. I really do want my leaving to be as amicable as possible.

I am tense, but calm.

I am ready to go. They tell me I can collect my case from the storeroom in a short while and that I can pack and say 'good bye'. This is unheard of. I can hardly believe what I am hearing. 'Big Brother thinks that is the right thing.' For one dreadful minute I think I may succumb. Remember Winston?

In the end Winston falls under the spell and LOVES BIG BROTHER.

Well, I wouldn't go that far. Though I admit I nearly did call that voice behind the makeshift wall 'Big Brother'. I am surprised by their decision and hope that it is a sign that the outside world has not entirely taken against me. I do not forget, however, that the production team is clever. They are setting the scene, hoping for a Big Brother moment. Knowing that I am going I could, if I were of another nature, go in to that bedroom and settle some scores.

They ask if there is a last thing I would like to say and I thank them for choosing me and for giving me the opportunity of experiencing this. I know that in some people's eyes I will have failed, and in a sense they are right, but in some games it is the one who walks away who is the ultimate winner.

I leave the Diary Room and walk in the garden while I wait for my cases. The team has asked if I think any one will miss me. I am certain they will not. Further, for some, my going will be a relief. They will be able to relax now and be themselves. This is particularly true of Carole, who I know has been inhibited by my presence. She loves being in the house and will love it even better with me gone. She is having the time of her life. I am not. I am a freer spirit but I doubt she will see it that way.

Later, much later, among the messages that are sent are two that sum up my feelings at that time. They do not have names so I cannot attribute them. They have seen me on the programme and wish to comment.

'As you get older you discriminate more and put up with less than you had to when you were young, you become more secure about yourself and less concerned about feeling the need to be liked or to fit in around those with whom you really have little in common with or cannot relate to. You measure situations more and weigh up the pros and cons and make decisions based on what will benefit you most. You also have the confidence and freedom to have greater convictions behind your beliefs and will not tolerate situations or people who irritate you as much. It's about knowing who you are and what you like or dislike and sticking to your principles more and setting firmer boundaries. Surrounded by 'drunken' screaming over excitable types just wanting to dance about (without music) and scream and bitch and obsess about their appearance it would drive me insane....'

My other correspondent put it rather more succinctly: THE OLDER YOU ARE THE LESS SHIT YOU ARE WILLING TO TAKE.

Both got it exactly right. Thank you.

In the garden I say goodbye to Gertrude. She won't thrive here, either.

I take the suitcase into the bedroom, turning on the main light as I go in so that the harsh light shines on to the late sleepers. All those mornings I have crept about, politely not waking anyone. I push aside some rags on the bench in the middle and open the case. The little grey case is inside. We are allowed to keep those cases. They, and my trophy from the breakdancing competition, are my souvenirs of my time in the Big Brother house. Someone asks where I am going and I tell them I am going home. It is impossible to convey the drama of all this to an onlooker. Within the house everything is magnified, especially comings and goings. I say that I am being allowed to pack my own case for which I am grateful and I think is an acknowledgement of how important that is to me. They know me so well. I hear Ziggy say to someone, 'She can stay here or in two hours she can be with her man.' A hole in one there, Ziggy.

Gerry sits by my case, crying. A drama queen. He touches my silk tunic, the one I didn't get to wear for eviction night, and my hand embroidered jacket from Afghanistan, with regret and longing. He would have liked me, he thinks.

Seany says he is sorry. I won't let him take credit for this leaving. No, it was all settled before last night, I tell them. I owe it to the others who will be the victims of Seany's 'pranks' to give him a warning. 'No, you aren't at all sorry. One of the irritating things about being in this house is that people do the most appalling things and think that by saying 'sorry' that it is all right. I put myself in that position last night. I won't put myself in it again.' One thing I am not in life is a victim.

It doesn't take a minute to pack the case. As I close it someone touches me on the back. 'Don't touch me. Don't touch me.' I don't know who it is but I do not wish to be touched by anyone. As I leave I hug some of them and say a few unplanned words. I hope they may remember just a little of me in the busy lives they will have ahead, but doubt it. I tell the twins to have a good time and to enjoy themselves. . 'You have been good friends.' I tell them that I shall look out for them and that in a few months they will never be out of the magazines. 'I shall be bored to tears with you and I shall say how I knew them when they were little and manky.' They laugh.

I bequeath my bed to Carole but I know she won't be having it. It wouldn't be in her carefully devised plan at all.

Dear Chanelle, all tousled and sleepy, will cry, as she cries over most things. I look at her. She is an ordinary girl pretending to be extraordinary but in spite of, or because of this, I sense that she will be one of the new 'celebrities'. I tell her I love her, which in that sentimental moment is true, and because I know she loves a good cry. Tracey says, 'see you in Newmarket,' which I find a bit sketchy. Nicky, good old Nicky, takes my case back to the storage room.

By the time I am back in the diary room I am a wrung rag. There is a last scene to be filmed. More going over old ground. Finally I am told to go through the door to my right. It opens and I am out and hand-held cameras are in my face and people lead me through black cardboard clad walls and I am in the open air and I am lead across a wide yard to a building and up some stairs to a small room.

I go to the window and look across at the 'house'. It is the first time I have seen it from outside. It is an enclosed space, all scaffolding and bits of this and bits of that like a shantytown. Makeshift and sad. It is Tenko. I was right. A prison camp.

People from the production team come to see me. I get no feel from them about what the reaction has been. I am adamant that no one, no one, is to come to collect me. I want to go home and I want to go home alone. They have sent for the psychiatrist. This is routine for everyone leaving the house. He brings pad and pen and settles down. There is nothing for me to say, 'I went in. I did not like it. I came out.' It won't make a thesis but I feel shut down towards him. He wants to talk to me about patronising the twins. I simply refuse to engage with him.

All I want is to know if everything is all right and I will only know this from David. They show me newspaper cuttings and tell me there is nothing to worry about. There has been very little coverage of me and what there is, is favourable. The producer comes and she is her usual self. No one will be able to tell me what I need to know. David is the only person who knows what I need to hear. A mobile is handed to me. It is David. 'Is everything all right?' I ask. He knows the breadth of the meaning behind the question. He and he alone will not lie to me. 'Yes,' he says. 'Everything is all right. I am very proud of you. We are all proud of you.' That is all I have ever needed to hear.

I am in control again. I tell him to stay put and he is to tell everyone else to do the same. A driver will get me home.

They bring my own suitcase. I use the bathroom and lock the door.

I sit drinking tea waiting for the driver. There is a flurry and Davina comes into the room. I had told Big Brother that my only regret in walking was that I would not meet Davina, which I had been told by the girls, was the 'best bit'. She tells me that she had begged Big Brother to go in to the house and have tea with me. She is absolutely lovely, totally charming and very good-looking. I can see why she is successful.

David says it is all right. The relief is totally overwhelming. Ziggy was right. 'She can stay here, or two hours and she can be with her man.'

Two hours later I am in Tetbury.

Two months later and I am still waiting to meet Andrew Marr.